At Home in t

At Home in the Elk River Valley

REFLECTIONS ON FAMILY, PLACE AND THE WEST

Mary B. Kurtz

First published by Dog Ear Publishing
4010 W. 86th Street, Ste H
Indianapolis, IN 46268
www.dogearpublishing.net

ISBN: 978-160844-944-6

This book is printed on acid-free paper.

Printed in the United States of America

"Having lived here for over twenty years, I thought I knew everything about the Elk River Valley. In Mary's memoir I discovered even more about the history and the people who settled here and those who followed. A great read for anyone who loves this special place."

—CJ Mucklow, *Routt County Extension Director, Colorado State University*

Photo Credits

Technical Photographic Assistance: Joel Schulman
Cover Photo: Mary B. Kurtz
Cover Design: Steamboat Design Associates
Proofreader: Emily Croom
Indexer: Teri Jurgens Lefever

"Tell me the landscape in which you live, and I will tell you who you are."

- Jose` Ortega y Gasset

Dedication

To Pete, Andy, and Cassidy; to the preservation of the inspiring landscape of the Elk River Valley; and to all pioneers, past and present, who courageously envisioned and pursued not only a different story line in the making of their own personal histories, but an enlightened future for the communities in which they lived.

Acknowledgements

One does not truly travel alone in the pursuit of researching and writing a book. Along the way I was fortunate to receive support from my family, friends, writing teachers, and volunteer readers. I could not have found my way with first drafts without the dedicated editing feedback from my husband, Pete. His straight- forward and honest critiques quickly pointed the way to a sharper truth in my writing. I want to thank my sister, Meg Spencer, for her early editing of my writing; my mother, Marguerite Bieber, and Alma Kurtz, my mother-in-law for their unfailing support and feedback on my manuscript.

When this collection of essays began to take shape, my writing teachers, Sharon Carmack and Sheila Bender, encouraged me to find and have faith in my voice; they asked me to persevere in re-writing drafts until they were truthful, clean, and revealing to the reader. Sharon helped me develop this manuscript as a whole and has played an invaluable role in editing and supporting the completion of this book. Sheila Bender first taught me about personal essays and also edited and critiqued my manuscript insisting on authenticity and clarity. I do not believe I would have remained committed to this project if it had not been for both Sharon's and Sheila's belief in my writing. To each of you, my deepest thanks.

The isolating practice of writing depends on the eyes and ears of others. I had a number of readers who, over the last four years, offered their time and feedback and in doing so helped my writing grow. They include: Nancy Reese Jones, a one-time resident of the

Elk River Valley, who read very early drafts of my essays and helped me clarify the initial direction of my writing; Jay Fetcher, whose work with the Cattleman's Land Trust was instrumental in preserving the land I write about; CJ Mucklow, Routt County Extension Agent, whom I write about and from whom I received unwavering support in writing about issues important to those who live not only in the Elk River Valley but throughout the West; Marsha Daughenbach, Executive Director of the Community Agricultural Alliance and third-generation cattle rancher, who helped me understand the importance of articulating the life we wish to preserve in our Western landscapes; and the following women, who, in their love of books and the land in which they live, offered me a renewed appreciation for the opportunity not only to live here but to write about the place I call home. Thank you, Leelee Wright, Jeannie Antrim, Michael Soward, Suzanne Speaker, and Louise Stafford, for your honesty, your enthusiastic support, and editorial expertise.

A number of individuals provided historical details, clarifications, and suggestions to my manuscript and I am grateful to each of them: Sharon Bedell, Judy Wetterberg, the late Kathy Main, Sarah Healey, Maureen Cole, Nancy Young, Gilbert Anderson, Steve Komfala, Chad Green, Jo Semotan, Dutch Bieber, Mary Burman, Junior Bedell, Susan Dorsey, Jay and Cynthia May, Judy Green, Connie Wagner, and Bobbi Beall.

With encouragement from Harriet Freiberger, I read my manuscript to the Steamboat Writer's Group during the winter of 2009 and 2010. The group's intelligent and candid feedback on my manuscript helped it take its final shape. Thank you to each of you for your personal and professional perspectives.

Author's Note

*A*t *Home in the Elk River Valley* is organized according to the seasons beginning with the spring of our arrival in the Elk River Valley. Within each season there are six essays with a short epigraph at the beginning of each essay. These epigraphs are diary entries from the period of time in which I wrote this book. While the epigraphs are seasonal they do not necessarily reflect the theme of the essay they introduce.

Table of Contents

Preface

My husband, Pete, and I came to the Elk River Valley in Colorado thirty years ago in our 1970 Ford pickup, nicknamed the "White Tornado." We longed for country living away from the busyness and encroachment of development in the small but popular western Colorado community of Glenwood Springs, where we lived in the late 1970s. Piled high with everything we owned, the dependable Ford delivered us to our new home, an old dairy barn and 120 acres, nestled in a small crook of the valley floor just north of Mad Creek. Built of square, rough-sawn logs in the 1940s and later renovated in the late 1960s, the historic dwelling had drawn us to a new life.

Two children and six years later, we moved north to a ranch near the banks of the Elk River, where our land encompasses ancient river bottom, meadowland, and oak-covered hillsides. Over the years, we have raised hay, Red Angus cattle, commercial elk, and performance quarter horses.

The dairy barn was a good start, and life on our ranch has been rich. As the nest emptied and quieted, I found myself in a midlife interlude, gathering the stories of the life my husband and I chose to live, reflecting on how our decisions shaped those stories, how parenting focused our living, and how both the natural world of our ranch and the contemporary world of our larger community challenged each one of us.

In this book I focused my writing and attention on both the raising and leave-taking of children, on the life of the ranch, on the natural world, and on the history of both family and the Elk River Valley. In witnessing my children's growth and independence, I am challenged by the conscious process of letting go, yet soothed by the strength that fills their flight of independence. In observing the return of the sandhill cranes from the Rio Grande and the wonderment of a newborn calf's drive to stand and nurse, I shared the same desires for the movement of the seasons, survival, and life itself. In remembering those whose footprints I have followed, I am made conscious of that which they have given me. And in recognizing that this Valley continues to draw and welcome new pioneers, I awaken to the task and need to protect and preserve the land and its history.

The reflections in *At Home in the Elk River Valley* celebrate family, place, and the West. They are a plea to all who read them to reflect on and preserve what is most cherished, past and present, within and without. As the historic preservationists have argued, understanding the past reminds us of what is important and informs us about how we might move into the future, marking a course for living well in the days ahead.

Mary B. Kurtz

Spring

The Cranes Return

Sandhill cranes in flight

Chapter One

The Cranes Return

Snows slip from granite steeps, trickling into crevices and creeks, merging with the Elk River, like an emigrant from the wilderness. Aspen and dogwood buds come to light. Jonquils, daffodils, and hyacinth fill twig baskets—imports from a greenhouse teasing those who thirst to pull the cover of snow back and walk in dew covered grass.

Spring 2005

I often hear the sandhill cranes before I see them. Today, just before noon, I see seven of them drift east overhead and then turn, circling the river. The flock rides leisurely on the rising current of warm air, circles for a few minutes, and then peels out of the thermal like a licorice string from its coil.

They head north, two cranes in tandem, and the remaining five flying one behind the other. I wonder if the two flying together aren't related, perhaps a parent flying with a young one, showing him the way, offering him encouragement if needed, the thermal just one stop on a tutorial flight. I watch until I can no longer see them. I imagine the late morning outing carrying on north, taking a left turn across the river, and landing at home again, on the low lying western banks of the river.

Sandhill cranes, a long-necked, long-legged species, trumpet like a French horn. With a wingspan of more than six feet, they fly dutifully in a V-formation from the Rio Grande to the Salmon River. They stop over in the San Luis Valley of southern Colorado on their way north in the early spring and on their way south come fall. Along the way groups drop off in summer nesting grounds near mudflats around reservoirs and moist agricultural areas, finding rich sources of food for survival and safety from human encroachment.

We used to see only one pair in the spring and think we were on safari in Africa witnessing a rare species. Now protected, they are common overhead with more nesting pairs finding adequate security and resources to claim their place in the Elk River Valley.

Just as the sandhill cranes sought safety in this valley for offspring yet to come, Pete and I also migrated here awaiting the arrival of our firstborn. Before settling in the Valley, I taught special education students the complex world of words, numbers, and social skills. The only horses I'd ever ridden were for my Girl Scout badge, one of a few sewn to my dark green sash. As a child I had, like some children, inexplicably imagined living in a landscape where winter lingers and the stunning mountain peaks tempt and nurture a person's spirit. The draw of the landscape in the Elk River Valley—the inherent sense of peace over its contours, the open invitation into relationship, the surety yet unforgiving strength of its seasons—drew me in with the lightest, yet unrelenting touch.

Pete, an entrepreneur, had owned a small real estate company and a hardware store. His family had been involved in a variety of agricultural operations in Western Colorado. He spent time in the company of horses from an early age. As a young man he dreamed of a farm or ranch of his own; he wanted to spend his days working in the out of doors, and he longed for his children to grow up in the company of animals and a natural landscape which they could explore.

So it was in 1979, with the help and opportunity of outside business interests, we chose to follow our idealism. We pulled *The Almanac for Rural Living* off the bookstore shelf to consider the practical challenges of self-sufficient living: solar energy and growing our own natural foods. In doing so, the dream of a different life began to take shape. We sought a place in which we would find an enduring connection to both a social and physical landscape. In the Elk River Valley we found both: small community living and an open and inspiring landscape for our family and the horses and livestock we would raise. We would follow in the footsteps of many before us.

Early pioneers and homesteaders who migrated to this valley also sought a safe haven: a land rich with food and resources for shelter. Over a century ago, they came into the Elk River Valley, entering the Yampa Basin from the east, perhaps through Buffalo Pass, or through Middle and North Parks following Ute Pass Trail due east of the Elk River's Slavonia and just south of Hahn's Peak. They first came seeking silver and gold, and then in search of the valley's grazing lands.

On word that gold had been discovered near the headwaters of the Elk River, prospectors came to Hahn's Peak in 1866. Some reports claimed "nuggets the size of walnuts" along Willow Creek. As with other gold seekers, the charge to mining claims was brisk and hopeful around Hahn's Peak. Mining claims named Bonanza, Black Nugget, Copper King, Golden Treasure, and Royal Flush boldly expressed the optimism of those panning for gold.

Then, as gold and silver mining activity began to decline in the late 1880s, a series of national events occurred that impacted the landscape of the valley below Hahn's Peak forever. It began with the Homestead Act of 1862, followed by railroad land grants and then the opportunity for free grazing on Public Lands. In addition, two economic panics sent many pioneers west, some to Routt County's rich agricultural areas. As activity in the Elk River Valley shifted from mining to homesteading and agriculture, the relationship between the pioneer and the land changed the character of the place for generations.

When the Homestead Act of 1862 passed, settlers could file for 160 acres of free land. The land was theirs at the end of five years, if they had built a house on it, dug a well, tilled at least ten acres, established a certain length of fencing, and occupied the dwelling. Settlers to the Elk River Valley eagerly claimed and established a piece of the landscape that would support a self-sustaining agrarian life. The pioneers found a rich soil for their crops. The meadow lands provided grazing for their sheep and cattle, and the free flowing Elk provided the water to sustain both their homesteading families and their newly developing agricultural endeavors.

Although beef, sheep, and hay production continue today in the Valley, as agricultural land has gradually become more valuable for development in a county with a large tourism base centered on skiing, outdoor recreation, and the western landscape, the economics of livestock and hay production have become more tenuous, even for the most financially astute rancher.

Pete and I listen now to the last whispers of family ranching dying out and see the evolution of land usage take its next step. In the Elk River Valley, a movement toward conservation easements began fifteen years ago. One by one, land owners have stepped forward in time by establishing conservation easements on their properties, giving up the right to develop their land for profit in exchange for state and federal tax benefits and ultimately preserving their land in perpetuity. Meadow lands will remain open for agricultural use. Subdivisions will not sidle up to the sandhill cranes' nesting ground, and a strip mall will never be my neighbor. Cherished physical landscape will remain much like the landscape homesteaders settled more than a hundred years ago.

We, like many, have been fortunate. In our thirty-one years in the Elk River Valley, we found community in the neighborhoods of Long Gulch, Smith Creek, and Dry Creek, as well as McPhee Draw, Sand Creek, Pearl and Steamboat Lakes. We found a deeply satisfying way of life in an often challenging western landscape. Day by day our family story was written through the daily comings and goings of parenting, ranching, participating in our rural community and the community of schools and volunteer organizations.

~~~

As the numbers of sandhill cranes have increased, I have more opportunity to watch the rare species fly overhead, their long bodies stretched as though they're reaching from the Elk to the Rio Grande. I follow their flight and feel connected, their flight infused with divinity. I am grateful for this gift of the sandhill cranes, for this land in which we have grown, and for those whose history and footprints we followed onto the banks of the Elk River.

Spring

Homesteaders

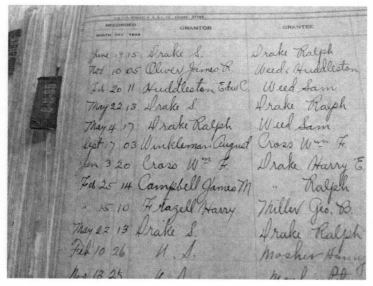

A page from the Routt County assessor's land records
documenting the names of Winkleman, Campbell, Drake, and Mosher

Chapter Two

Homesteaders

*Petite purple crocuses erupted overnight, a surprise
every year. One day they're covered in snow, and the
next thing I know I spot them out of the corner of my
eye, beneath the kitchen window. A diminutive group-
ing, I wish I could save the pocket-sized crocus; they
come and go so quickly. I'm afraid I haven't cherished
their moment of surprise: they, just a wink each
spring.*

Spring 2005

In mid-April when the mud deepens and life
outside begins to emerge, Pete, Andy, our
neighbor and general contractor, and Bryan, the soils
test engineer, stand over a test hole in front of the old
cabin, leaning on their shovels like a road crew, talking about ground water and sewers.

Bryan's soils' testing is just the beginning of
rebuilding the original homestead house on the
ranch. While the homestead had a long and storied
history, it was full of wildlife, both in its walls and
under its partial cinderblock foundation. Its four
walls had quite literally become part of the natural
web of life, providing housing for mice, snakes,
skunks, and an occasional fox. Building a new structure on the imprint of the old had become essential.

Just as I walk closer to the conclave, curious to
learn more about the world of dirt and sewers
and county regulations, a red pickup turns in the

driveway with a For Sale sign in the window. Pete quickly let me know, "Oh, that's Kirby. He's coming to get Nate." Pete excuses himself from the soils testing work and walks over to Kirby's truck, the busyness not unusual when the winter retires. Everyone sheds winter by getting out, taking a drive, checking in on friends, and starting new projects.

Kirby Blackman and his wife, Dottie, rented the old cabin for twelve years, before leaving for Cody, Wyoming, last fall. They'd become family. Kirby moved everything up to their new place except Nate, a red roan with a personality much like Kirby's.

Kirby's long legs slide easily out of the truck cab. He stands as he usually does, loosely, hands in the front pockets of his Wranglers, belt loops empty, wearing a western cotton shirt with snap buttons, and cuffs always unsnapped because Kirby's arms are so long. He announces in a deep, slow voice, "Well, I came to get that redhead, if you haven't shot him yet."

Pete teases, "As a matter of fact, we got a really good price at the killer's just last week." They both chuckle and understand that neither one of them would send Nate to the slaughter house. Kirby thought Nate might be with us for just a couple of months when he left. Now that it's April, he's uncomfortable, feeling that Nate's overstayed his welcome. Kirby always preferred to be on the other side of helping people out. Kirby's smile appears, partially hidden beneath his bushy, droopy mustache, and he shakes his head. "I wouldn't blame ya. What a knot head."

Then Kirby notices the sewer activity and wonders what we're doing with the old place he rented from us. "So what are you up to?"

"We're tearing the old cabin down, Kirby."

Kirby looks at Pete, bewildered. He never thought there was anything wrong with the old house, not the annoying nuisances of something old, like freezing pipes in February or low water pressure in the summer, because the roping steers needed water in the corral below his kitchen. It suited both Dottie and him just fine. They got up in the morning to go to work and came home at night to a cozy gas-fired heater, radiating heat from a corner of the dining room in the middle of the house. He worked as a policeman, and Dottie worked in town too, for the Visiting Nurses Association. She studied for her bachelors and then her masters in that house. Kirby didn't think she'd ever get done. But she did. Then Cody, Wyoming, inherited two people who would help anyone—people who typify the West in their independence, self-sufficiency, and goodwill.

Perhaps Kirby's comfort in the old cabin goes back to its beginnings, to the spirit of those who settled here. The history of the old cabin began in the late 1800s when homesteading pioneers first moved into the Elk River Valley, finding the river bottom perfect for raising sheep. Several early homesteaders, including Hank Campbell, a Dutchman by the name of Winkleman, and the Mosher family claimed rights to parcels of land that make up the land on which our ranch now rests. In the recorded history it appears the Mosher family, actually built the original homestead cabin and ran a dairy operation here until they sold out their parcel to Ralph Drake in 1933.

Then in 1934, Ralph Drake sold this portion of land to Harlan Powell, and for the next twenty-seven years, the Powell family ran sheep here and eventually passed the ranch down to the next generation through a sale from father to son. In 1961, Travis and Bernice Arnett purchased the ranch and owned it until 1968, when they sold it to their daughter Sharon and her husband, Orval Bedell. This sale and transfer of land from father to a son or daughter marked a time when transferring agricultural land and a way of life to the next generation was not only financially practical but a natural way for families to weave the lives and livelihoods of children, fathers, and grandfathers together.

Sharon's family had roots in Nebraska, while Junior's family had long lived in the Elk River Valley. They both stand close to the earth. Sharon's eyes meet yours as though she wants you to know just exactly who she is and what she thinks. Beneath Oval's ("Junior" to everyone around here) snap cowboy shirt, you see the high school wrestler, rancher, roper, horse trainer, and father of a World Champion Steer Wrestler: the small but strong shoulders, the once steely chest, and the face lined with winters feeding with hay wagons drawn by draft horses and shoeing ten horses a day in August's late summer heat.

In the years when Junior and Sharon wintered in Jensen, Utah and summered here, they pastured their sheep, and Junior shod horses, roped with friends, and turned out a steer in the bucking chute for one of the boys to ride when the chores were done. In the quiet of those years after their boys left home, their marriage came to an end. Although their place was lost, Sharon and Junior set aside one hundred acres on the western border of the ranch, a tie to the collective memories of the family and the meaning they once found in calling this river bottom their summer home. Today the one hundred acres provide their sons, Chad and Travis, pasture for their horses, a small crop of oats, and sites for two homes. Junior's youngest son, Travis, has just finished building a home of his own on the property where he will raise his young son, Luke Orval, a namesake to his grandfather.

Ranches will continue to trade hands and the new owners will not necessarily be the next generation of ranching families. Inheritance tax laws make it difficult, if not impossible, to transfer the land to the next generation. The value of a rancher's estate is usually tied directly to the value of the land. When his or her children settle the estate, they most often have to sell the ranch to pay for the estate taxes, which can equal as much as 50 percent of the estate's value.

Often the next generation also realizes that the challenges of making an agricultural operation profitable, if it's not already owned free and clear, can be overwhelming. The price range for agricultural lands in our county is from $10,000 an acre to more than $20,000. In order to be profitable, a rancher needs to buy land priced at $500 an acre or own the ranch and infrastructure debt free, which is rarely the case. Unfortunately, living on the land here, and in many areas in the United States, no longer means a relationship with the land dependent on a reasonable value for cultivating it.

While the stories of beginnings and endings will continue to fill the history of the Elk River Valley, they will include changes in the way those who live here interact with the landscape. When Kirby came to the place, he and Dottie wanted to settle in the quiet of the Valley. They wanted to be near the high mountain ranges for hunting and trail riding. They wanted the peace that comes from living just close enough to your neighbors that you can see a porch light in the distance. And they came to the old cabin because the friends they knew lived along the same river.

We purchased the ranch from Sharon and Orval in 1985. Our tenure on this land has challenged us through the work of all seasons. Its natural beauty and intimate neighborhood have nurtured both our children and us. We relished sharing the river bank with Kirby and Dottie while they were here and now enjoy the company of new renters, two newcomers from Michigan, who have also found comfort in their home in the Elk River Valley. We are grateful to have followed in the footsteps of those before us: Hank Campbell, Mr. Winkleman, the Moshers, the Drake brothers, Sharon and Junior, and others.

When the old cabin comes down in June, I realize its history will be forgotten if it's not shared. Perhaps a small, framed note placed just inside the front door of the new house, tracing the history of the old cabin, might be a reminder to those who move in of those whose footprints rest beneath theirs.

This log cabin was built in 2007 on the site of the ranch's original homestead cabin, which was built in the early 1900s by the Mosher family. The original cabin was constructed of square timbers harvested from forests burnt by the Ute Indians to discourage white settlers. Over the years the homestead and cabin were owned by sheep ranchers and dairymen including the Drakes, the Moshers, the Powells, the Arnetts, and the Bedells. For those who call this cabin home, we hope the Elk River Valley will both inspire and comfort you while you are here.

As we look forward to tearing down the homestead cabin and building back up again, we embrace our thirtieth spring in the Elk River Valley. The song birds will return as they always do; miniature wildflowers in white, yellow, and blue will peek out from beneath the cottonwoods; and as the moon continues to greet us in the eastern sky, the river will rise.

We will save the old windows and doors for our own use or to give to the housing recycle business that started up not long ago. The track hoe will roll in before the aspens leaf out, and in a few giant grasps, the old cabin will become a pile of discarded lumber, dry wall, siding, and linoleum flooring. The site will be scraped clean, and excavation for the new log cabin will begin. One by one the logs will be stacked one upon the other until the cabin walls rise again. When complete and filled with new Elk River inhabitants, it will be their footprints that will carry along the history of our valley, creating the next collection of settlers' stories.

Spring

Spring's Dance

Mother and calf deep in hay

Chapter Three

Spring's Dance

The daffodils peek out from the moist earth and look back at me tentatively. A fine sugar dusting of snow blankets the barn roof as we await four more foals to run with the others. How I want to push through this wet spring. Then as I linger, I remember book titles like The Power of Now *and* Loving What Is *and nudge myself to take in a tardy spring in all its gray, wet, and cool.*

Spring 2005

Last week, we brought the cows in, back to their calving ground. The lumbering mothers moved steadily, their pregnant bellies jostling side-to-side. On horseback, Pete and I moved the small herd of thirty—many fewer than the 130 or so we used to carry—onto the road from their winter feeding ground. They took the first turn out of the gate and moved homeward. We always hope they keep their noses headed in the right direction. If they've done it before, memory of their calving ground guides their hoof-steps. But this group has an independent and free-spirited cow in the lead. She's temporarily forgotten the place where she gave birth. Following her lead down the road, the herd took the first possible turn off the main county road, right over a cattle guard.

Pete swore loud enough for them to hear, "You stupid bitches!"

All cowboys know their angry words will just sail into the wind, as the cows run and kick on up the neighbor's driveway anyway. But Pete hollered again and raced around the cattle guard to get ahead of that lead cow.

Our work was cut out for us now. Moving small numbers of cattle is like putting mercury back in the thermometer. Most ranchers will attest, there aren't many "easy buttons" in their work place. I went on up ahead to get a small group out of another neighbor's yard and worked carefully to hold them on the road as I waited for Pete's wandering ladies. Once he pushed them up to meet my group, he looked back to see five cows that turned back unannounced.

We watched as they ran lickety split up the fence line—on the *other* side of the fence line—as confused and irrational as mice trapped in an unfamiliar maze. Pete let loose again, as he spurred his horse to cut them off and turned them into the fence. He screamed at the lead cow, "You wild old bitty, get back there. Yah!" Once out of the main gate, they gave in a bit and headed down the road, thankfully cooperating, now out of breath from their frenzied spree.

With the small herd now settled into the mile walk to the ranch's main meadow, Pete and I relaxed in our saddles with the excitement of our small, but chaotic round-up over. Back at home, the herd wandered easily onto the meadow and headed out following their instincts to water, feed, or rest. In a few weeks, the meadow will begin to green, and the calves will nap in leftover hay from the morning feeding.

As we keep an eye on the weather and the herd, they huddle up against a few scrub oaks by the road as they do when a storm is moving in. There's a bit of grass for grazing and they're protected from the wind under the scraggly brush. I imagine them as eager as I, waiting for spring and their babies.

Low-pressure systems bringing storms help. They have a way of bringing on more births. For a rancher whose herd is calving, it's a wonderful mixed blessing. First, you know to expect some babies during the pending stormy weather. You can prepare to watch more carefully for your heifers, the herd's first-time moms. But you also worry. A calf can freeze to death in a spring storm if it can't get out of the wet and cold. Most mothers do a fine job of licking their babies off so they dry. But some mothers don't, and a calf born during a wet storm may face a rough start.

I have often watched as a cow lies in the cold, dead grass all by herself, her isolation a possible sign of labor. I hope her labor will be quick and efficient, the contractions hard and fruitful. Restlessly she gets up and down; she stands to take a few steps and then lies down again, her head stretched out on the ground as though she relinquishes herself to the wonderment of birth.

If the cow's older, labor and birth come more quickly. Once the calf is on the ground, the cow stands to lick her newborn, removing the birthing sac, first from the baby's head, and then licking the rest away. Steam rises from the afterbirth and wet newborn. The calf's head will rise and fall before it begins to stay up, wobbling from side to side before holding steady.

The drive for survival powers the calf to gather her legs under her and make the leap to stand, wobbly and disoriented. Mom continues to lick and encourage as the dance begins: up to try to nurse, down again to rest, and mom calmly follows: nose to nose, breath to breath. A few minutes pass by and they're up again, mom nudging the calf to find her milk. The calf, still tipsy, finds mom's bag and makes several passes at her udder before grabbing on. The calf reminds me of kids in Halloween costumes bobbing for apples, trying to grab onto a moving target. The calf finally finds the mother's teat and gets its first milk, life-saving colostrum.

Observing, I feel as though I'm a birthing doula, a woman trained to assist, support, and witness the wonderment of a new life. I understand the dance between the mother and baby, the mirroring of movement, the finely tuned attention, and constant hovering. The attachment is deep and will only deepen in the days ahead. The breathing, the licking, and the mimicking create a bond that will insure mother and baby won't lose one another when they get separated, once they return from the birthing ground and join the herd. Pete and I still stand amazed after branding in the spring, when a large herd of cows is rejoined with their babies; each mother can smell and find her own uniquely scented baby.

Although I don't find my babies, my children, by scent, I understand. I always feared getting separated from my children: shopping with pre-schoolers in the mall; worrying about adolescents driving home on icy roads or on California highways; watching my competitive son and daughter riding fast, wild horses; imagining fleeing shadows of predators, burglars, and scary things in the night outside their apartment window. I feared a breaking of the bond, the physical and emotional connection. I too worried and searched, just as the mother cow wandered and searched for her calf until she found her offspring and they were made whole again, their dance renewed.

Spring

The Bull Sale

The Northwest Colorado Bull Sale
From left, Marsha Daughenbaugh, Bill Gay, Troy Allen, and Terry Jost

Chapter Four

The Bull Sale

Cottonwood shadows fall long over the meadow. Sun brings daybreak to the ridge behind Deep Creek. Then clouds delay morning's rise in the aspen and oak brush nearby. I wonder, where will I stand today, in the shadows or the light?

Spring 2005

I crush saltines into my chili, wishing they were Fritos, and perhaps unconsciously desiring a richer mixture of fat and salt. I think to myself, my amygdala, my old brain, is telling me to prepare for survival in the cold fairgrounds arena, even though the arctic season is fading and the sun is setting higher over the silos dotting the hillside to the west.

It's always cold in the sale barn in early April, and we Routt County Cattlewomen know it. So we serve chili, brownies, and lots of hot coffee. Balancing my styrofoam bowl with the cellophane packages of saltines, I stop to chat with the ladies serving the chili. "How's it going? Do you have enough chili? Do you need any help?" Everything is great. They have enough brownies for two sale days instead of one, but they've run out of cheese and salad. Turnout gets bigger every year. We're surprised but cautiously encouraged. Maybe cattle producers aren't dying out after all.

The sale bulls passively wait: washed and brushed, resting in their honeycombed pens, inured to their captivity. Buyers walk up and down the arena, looking for bulls that will fit their breeding programs. Some might need a bull for their cows; some might need a smaller bull for their heifers (yearling cows). Sixty-five yearling bulls and three pens of replacement heifers, young cows used to replace older culled cows, wait their turn on the auction block. One by one they'll be led to the auction ring and purchased by a rancher who desires their unique genetics, their ability to pass along maternal characteristics to their daughters, newborns who calve easily, and animals who grow to weights that bring in critical profits.

The earthy smell of the sale pen belies the technology and the economic considerations of the cattle industry and the bidding ranchers. After many years of standing next to cattle, my mind continues, uncontrollably, to square the proof these bulky, pungent creatures transmute into a rancher's financial survival.

Pete and I sort through a few bulls looking for a heifer bull; the sale program gives us all the statistics cattlemen look for: EPDs, expected progeny differences; how likely the desired traits of the bull will be passed on to his progeny; birth weights and weaning weights. We find a couple of bulls, but we prefer to purchase a Red Angus bull, and these are Black Angus bulls. I hear Pete, "You know, if the price were right, I might take one home. We really need a bull." I'm surprised that Pete considers it. His preference for Red Angus has always been strong, rooted in wanting something unique, something that sets his cattle production apart and communicates a product made with care on a small scale. He struggles not to weaken against the popularity of the Black Angus breed.

The DNA of Black Angus and Red Angus cattle line up like twisty twin helixes. Genetically, both breeds are identical except for a recessive gene that determines the red color in the Red Angus breed. But the West prefers black; buyers pay up to two to three dollars more per one hundred pounds for Black Angus. The "Certified Angus Beef" brand was created in 1978 by the American Angus Association as a marketing tool to sell more Angus bulls. To qualify, cattle must be predominantly (51 percent) black. So, Red Angus producers have and will continue to sell in a disadvantaged marketplace.

I, too, prefer Red Angus. My irrational attachment to red may match the Western cattleman's to black, but my eye is warmed rather than repelled by the burnt sienna of the Red Angus mother and young fresh calf at her side. I fancy the earth rising and warming on the back of the Red Angus as I look across our herd, whether the day is the equinox or the winter solstice. We will stick with red knowing the market price may very well be less than if the cattle we ship in November were black. The urge to stand apart with our Red Angus herd, as a few other local ranchers do too, feels as old as the West.

The livestock auction clatters along, like they all do, with a chatter and buzz that push aside the fine dust rustled up by leather boots and cloven hooves. Whimsical neighbors inquire, "How's your mud?" It's always a question neighbors can commune over, not so much a competition of who has more, but of sharing the frustrations of winter's thaw. A welcome but sticky moist earth can linger in this part of the country until Mother's Day, sucking rubber boots right off.

Then fondness replaces humor, and they ask, "How's the kids? Where's that boy of yours?" They know Andy, "that boy of ours" because they helped him judge livestock in the county 4-H program, or they watched him show his Hampshire and Duroc pigs during fair.

We'll ask about their kids, too. "Hey, how's Tucker getting along at school? Is he going to transfer to Colorado State?"

Then we're faced with a passage of time we're not ready for when we run into 4-H kids we once knew who are married and now parents. We're surprised to see them holding a baby or following around an eighteen month old. "Chad, when did this happen? Who's this?" And he says, "Oh, this is Carter." And we watch both parents smile at Carter and smile at each other and then look our way with another smile. The time that filled those years folds like an accordion, a construction paper fan, and I am at once here and then there, fifteen years ago, the present and the past all one moment as I try to steady myself.

Andy followed Chad Green around the livestock judging circuit when he was in high school. Chad showed Andy how to laugh about being a ranch kid and how to think about animals. Chad married Kacey, the livestock judging coach at the University of Wyoming and they returned to help manage Chad's family ranch. Chad's parents, Bill and Ramona Green, moved to The Dry Fork Ranch, just north of Craig, Colorado, in 1978. On open range, irrigated meadows, and hillsides covered in service berries, oak brush, and sage brush, the Green family raises cattle, in addition to a few registered cows with which to raise their own breeding bulls, and opens their ranch to deer and elk hunters during the fall season. Chad also hires out as an auctioneer, primarily for county fair livestock auctions. Today, Chad will auctioneer the bull sale. By hiring Chad (and other young local auctioneers like Troy Allen in the essay photo), the agricultural community loyally supports the next generation.

Steadying a cup of hot chocolate to cut the chill, we take our seats half-way up the bleachers and settle in. Chad, his hat resting at a bold cowboy slant, begins by introducing himself and the two ring men who watch for bids from the hands and eyes of the bidders. One of them, Dean Vogelaar, grew up on a farm in Kansas and always wears his Wranglers with suspenders. He has an easy hello for anyone he meets, loves to trail ride on his loyal gray horse, and assures customers at a locally owned bank where he works that their money is in good hands.

The help in the ring can only do their job with help from any number of cowboys and cowgirls in the back, moving the bulls out of the pens and through the chutes, the sturdy lumbering bodies banging and shifting the chute panels as they go. With a stock stick in hand, the cowboys and cowgirls poke and encourage all the forward movement they can, accompanying their push with a "Hey, get up there. C'mon let's go. Move it."

The bulls line up to enter the ring, the ground from the arena stirs and rises: the sand, the manure, and the pungent odors from live animals create a thin but palatable, organic haze. Each bull is usually hand-led by an owner or handler who's been asked to help out. Around the ring they go, moving out to show off the bull's frame: his top line, a fine ratio between bone and muscular growth, and small shoulders for easy birthing of his offspring. Ranchers consider what they see in the ring with the bull's EPD numbers, calf birthing and weaning weights; and what they need to improve their own breeding program. They may need a big muscular bull to put weight on lighter cows or they may need a smaller bull for their heifers.

Chad gives out a shout, "Hey, all right here, what do ya' want to give? Looky here, looky here, what ya' want to give me? Give me $3000, bid 'em on $3000 now.

Give me, give me, $3000. Looky here now, I'll let you in at $1500, fifteen now, bid 'em on fifteen. Dean, what have you got? Got fifteen, got fifteen? Give me fifteen."

Dean quickly raises his hand high in the air pointing to his bidder and shouts out, "Ya!" and the air fills with the inherent sense of competition that auctions spur and require.

Chad continues, "Now sixteen, now sixteen, hey, bid 'em, bid 'em sixteen, now give me sixteen."

If the bidding begins to lag, Chad, like all good auctioneers, sells the crowd, "Hey now, you can't buy this bull any day of the week. He's got the looks, the performance, and EPDs that would help anyone's breeding program. Come on now, what ya' give me? Give me sixteen, give me sixteen."

The sale seems brisk: just enough buyers and interest in the pool of bulls for sale that the bidding carries along reasonably well. Whether a rancher is looking for similar genetics for his herd or a genetic change for hybrid vigor, the bulls are selling at market prices.

Pete and I wait for the one bull we finally decided on from our bull sale sheet. If they go for a good price, we'll consider one. If they go for a much higher price, our reluctance to place Black Angus in our herd will win out and we'll go home with an empty trailer.

Lot #22 walks in the ring. We still like what we see as Chad starts up the bidding. "Hey, look now, we've got a nice young bull with the frame and muscle to work for you. What ya' give me? Fifteen, fifteen, let me hear fifteen." We aren't the only ones who like Lot #22. The bidding moves up quickly, and Pete and I realize the bull will go for more than we are willing to pay. Now, we will have to continue our search elsewhere for the right bull.

Climbing down off the bleachers, we feel empty handed. Chad's mesmerizing auctioneer's chant sings out over the stands as his gavel rhythmically hits the auctioneer's stand. "Hey, what ya' give me, now?" Nearly all sixty-five yearling bulls would sell and one pen of heifers would go home with a new owner. The animals that did not sell were either not what the buyers wanted or didn't bring the price the seller had imagined. We wonder to ourselves, perhaps ranching is surviving in northwestern Colorado. Perhaps the bull sale does provide an important resource to local beef producers who continue to hang on to their enterprises.

As the late afternoon shadows gather and the air begins to chill, Pete and I pile into the warmth of the pickup. Even though we didn't find the right bull at the annual sale and the trailer is empty, we find ourselves renewed. Heading home we feel the spaces created by winter's still months fill with the stories of friends unseen and unheard since the first snow. In them we find ourselves connected again, to our past and our children and to life's ever-strong heartbeat in the faces of newborns and the young. In them we find a comforting reminder that our rural life, the agricultural rituals of the season, and the long-held connections between our family and others we've known nourish and sustain us.

Spring
Chico's Wild Roots

Pete and Andy training in the arena

Chapter Five

Chico's Wild Roots

A lone elk makes her way across our meadow and back up the hillside, going home after a trip to the river for water. I'm curious. Elk usually make their way in groups. Often they retreat to the hillside as though pursued by the law; cautiously they make their way across the meadow, leaping fence lines, and darting here and there as they scoot through the oak brush. But this peaceful animal takes her time foraging on new grass, ambling through the oak, finding a new way home, as if returning from a meditation at river's edge.

Spring 2005

The barn light was on when I wandered in the dark to bed last night. That usually means someone forgot to turn it off. I crawled into bed thinking Pete will take care of it, as he usually does every night: I, like a sleepy child, depending on someone else to take care of the world.

The next morning I tell Pete the lights were left on in the barn. "Not all night, they weren't."

"But they were on when I went to bed."

He asks, as if knowing the answer, "Are you sure?"

"Well, I think so."

He reassures me, "I turned them off after you went to bed. I'm tricking Chico into thinking it's spring."

In preparation of finding a buyer for Chico, a nine-year old dun quarter horse, Pete exposes him to extra hours of artificial light, signaling Chico's pituitary gland to shed his heavy wool coat, producing a slick smooth coat early in the spring. With Chico's athletic build and dun color, Pete hopes that, just like he and Andy did years ago, buyers will swoon over a slicked off dun, reminiscent of man's enduring and historic admiration for the horse.

A dun, often mistakenly called buckskin, may vary in color between buttermilk and copper penny; Chico's a golden dun. He too possesses the signature dorsal stripe of a dun, suggesting to old-time horsemen the horse's genes reach deep into the gene pool, a tie embraced and admired in dun horses. Despite their size, all horses, wild or domesticated, are a predator's prey in the natural world. Cowboys and westerners ascribe to the dun a potent and admirable instinct to survive.

A neighboring rancher had sold Chico to our son, Andy, for $950. Both Andy and Pete loved Chico's mother and speculated a baby of hers would make a great roping horse. Big and stout, Chico grew to stand 15½ hands and weighs 1,200 pounds. His size and athletic build would help haul steers around, once a roper threw a loop and dallied the steer to his horn.

But over the years Chico's inconsistent nature remained challenging to Pete and Andy. One day he would be focused, dependable, intelligent. The next day he would act like a perfect two year old: eager, but fearful; cooperative, but driven by primitive instincts to independence.

The domestication of horses is a relatively modern development. It began on the steppes north of the Black Sea three to four thousand years ago when horses were harnessed like oxen for driving. A few hundred years before Christ's birth, the Greek Xenophon wrote the first training manual on the riding horse. Unlike the authors of Greek mythology, Xenophon encouraged man to understand the "psyche" of the horse. Xenophon believed a horse that understood and trusted the actions of his rider would work with confidence. Most importantly, Xenophon believed mutual respect was essential between horse and rider.

A retired doctor, Sharon Gulley, asked Andy to work with her horse one summer. While she sat on her horse, the two discussed how horses think and how riders need to understand the relationship between their actions and their horse's response. The next time she came for a training session, Sharon brought Andy one of her favorite books on horses: *The Art of Horsemanship* by Xenophon.

Around 350 B.C. Xenophon wrote:

> When one has bought a horse that he really admires, and has taken him home, it is a good thing to have his stall in such a part of the establishment that his master shall very often have an eye on the animal...the man who neglects this matter is neglecting himself for it is plain that in moments of danger the master gives his own life into the keeping of his horse.

In Xenophon's manual he goes on about the importance of handling horses with gentleness and understanding:

> The one precept and practice in using a horse is this – never deal with him when

you are in a fit of passion. When your horse shies at an object and is unwilling to go up to it, he should be shown that there is nothing fearful in it, least of all to a courageous horse like him; but if this fails, touch the object yourself that seems so dreadful to him, and lead him up to with gentleness. Compulsion and blows inspire only the more fear.

Having never heard of Xenophon, we were all intrigued first and foremost by the period in which he lived and what he understood about horses at the time. Much of his understanding was lost for centuries. Reading his manual was like reading about both the Native Americans' respect for and devotion to their horses and contemporary thought and practice in horse training, which only recently evolved from a harsh, authoritarian view of taming wild broncs. Often wranglers on large ranches did, and still do bring in young or wild horses to a pen, halter them, hold them, and control them, if need be, with physical force. I imagine Xenophon sitting on the top rail of the pen, wondering how man could take so many steps backwards, go deaf and cold, ignoring a horse's deepest nature, and ultimately create a horse under saddle also deaf and cold to the cowboy's communication and direction.

Pete and Andy gratefully follow in Xenophon's footsteps. The intricacies of horse training and horsemanship are at the forefront of Pete and Andy's day. "Dad, did you try Fappani's exercise on the counter canter?" "Hey, Andy, I tried that tear-drop snaffle (a second stage early training bit) on Dudley, and he really got soft." The horse training magazines and industry publications cover our TV room couch and the kitchen counter. They're saved in a large woven basket, just in case the perfect exercise is needed down the road for a particular problem with a young horse.

After several attempts to sell Chico during the early days of spring, Pete runs across a cowboy who buys and sells horses whenever he finds one he likes: a modern-day horse trader. Jeff loves looking at Chico: his dun color, his dark stripe, his stout athletic confirmation and deep chest; all hallmarks of a cow-boy's ideal roping horse.

Standing out in the barn yard, the guys chat back and forth about horses and roping. Jeff comes back to Chico, "You know he's pretty darn nice, Pete. What'll you'll take for him?"

"Well Jeff, I know he's worth more as a roping horse, but I'll take $4,000 if you like him."

Jeff turns to Pete, "Sounds fair to me. I'll take him."

Pete always wants buyer and seller to feel square with one another when the trailer door closes and the new owner drives down the driveway. And that day he felt satisfied.

Jeff finds a buyer shortly after he and Chico leave our place: a neighbor, who, unknown to us, needs a new roping horse. Once on Chico, he, like Pete and Andy, loves Chico's heart, desire, and will-ingness to track (follow) a steer. Chico is the roping horse our neighbor has always hoped to load up for the next roping in town. In Chico, he has a strong horse, a smart horse, the brave and loyal horse he has always admired. In the days ahead, we learn that our neighbor succeeds in finding the mental and emo-tional point where both he and Chico could exist—the two of them in silent communication, as they exploded from the roping chute together.

***

Even though Chico's new owner looked forward to this new working relationship with optimism, he, unfortunately, would be robbed of it unexpectedly in just a few short months. One afternoon without warning, Chico colicked, his intestines doubling over, twisting, causing him the kind of pain he cannot escape nor endure. Colic in horses is not unusual, but sometimes even with prompt intervention and medical care, horses die in a few hours. After two days of medical attention, Chico loses his battle and leaves our neighbor without the horse in which he found a kind of Wild West communion. Chico leaves us, too, with the knowledge that even the strong and the brave are vulnerable.

Spring
Branding

The Kurtz Ranch Brands: Spear Quarter Circle
and Two Quarter Circle

Chapter Six

Branding

The wind chimes ring out. The sun rises, making its way from Dublin, Montreal, Duluth, and Mountain Home. Soon it will brush the willows and pine tops; soon it will light my paper and warm my eyes: a traveling spirit, posing as fire in the sky.

Summer 2005

When the tulips under the kitchen window billow, it's branding time on the ranch. Each year in early May we gather the cows and calves from their peaceful life on the spring meadows and move them into the corrals behind the barn. This gathering can be a simple matter or it can be morning of struggle and cursing.

The bawling and protestations begin as soon as we walk around behind the herd on horseback and begin to drive them toward the open gate by the corrals. At least one high-strung cow will sense trouble immediately and high tail it in the other direction, leaving her calf disoriented and struggling to follow or sometimes completely abandoned. At that moment, Pete takes off in her direction, yelling back at me, "I'll get that one. You stay with the others. Just push 'em up against the fence." And off he goes, spurring his horse over the irrigation ditch, headed for the scrub oak below the road where the cow seems to head for cover. Pete's determination and fearlessness on his horse always surpasses the mother cow's.

He always wins out, usually with the help of a third rider who closes off an open space in the meadow and allows Pete to drive the cow back to the herd where I'm walking them along the fence line.

With the herd gathered, we begin again to move them down the fence line, through the gate, down the alley-way and into the corrals. One by one, we separate the cows from their babies, sending the cows out into a holding area and moving the calves into a smaller corral. When it comes to the actual branding routine, we've used a number of techniques to gather up the calves. We've followed in the footsteps of traditional brandings and used a horse and rider to rope each calf and drag it to the branding area, where additional hands grab the calf and hold it down. We've pushed the calves down our alley and into a calf chute where they are restrained. And finally, when we work with our calves in small groups, which we often do, friends and family jump in and help grab a calf by a hind leg and drag it to a working area by the barn door where we have vaccines, ear tags, and a branding iron ready.

It takes two hands to manage a calf. One holds a hind leg and the other grabs the calf's head. Together, the two hands sit down on the ground. The hand at the rear of the calf stretches it out pushing the other hind leg as far forward as possible, while the second hand sits on the neck of the calf and pulls back a front leg. A third hand handles the vaccines and ear tags; and a fourth hand, usually Pete, castrates the bull calves and brands the calf. Those on the ground hold the calf tight. A hundred pound calf can put up a fight that gives even the strongest help a beating as the calf's legs kick wildly for release. Vaccinations are administered first for common calf diseases and pink eye. Then Pete puts the branding iron carefully on the left hip, pressing down hoping the calf won't move. The searing iron burns through the hair, crackling and smoking on its way to the skin. The pungent smell of burnt hair quickly permeates all one's clothing and senses and is not easily escaped nor forgotten.

If the calf moves, the branding iron may slip and distort the image. Pete strives for a clean brand each time just as a graphic artist strives for clarity in a commercial design. A brand indicates ownership and when the day comes to sell the calf, the identity of the brand needs to be clear for the brand inspector to read it. So, if the brand is clean, a small celebration follows, "Hey, good one." Or, a satisfying, "That'll do." If the help on the ground gets yanked by a large calf and Pete slips with the branding iron, there's immediate cursing in the branding banter. A hand on the ground shouts out "Holy crap! That's a rowdy one. Get back here you little shit." And as Pete steps back to get out of the way, "Damn it, not again. Hold on now, I gotta get this right."

In the middle of such a long-held ranching tradition every spring, Pete and I never fail to feel as though there were a more humane way to brand cattle. Our ambivalence never finds a satisfying alternative. The branding of cattle in the state of Colorado is state law, so we must carry on with our chore each year.

So, one by one we work our way through the herd of young calves. When we're finished, we push the calves out to the holding area where their mother's eagerly await, having never given up bawling for their babies return. Once mothers and babies are together, we push them back onto the meadows by horseback, the return drive to open spaces orderly and quiet. Our branding day ends with a sense of satisfaction; the physical labor, the coordinated work of many hands, and the eventual reuniting of mothers and their babies at the end of the day sounds out a deep reminder of a natural rhythm to the world.

We won't think much about our Two Quarter Circle brand until late fall when we get ready to sell our calves. Sometime in November Pete will give a local livestock shipper, Neil Chew, a call and ask him when he can take a load to the Centennial Livestock Auction in Fort Collins. Each spring, Neil's family brings their sheep and cattle into North Routt County to graze in the high country and return them come late November to their home place in eastern Utah near Jensen. They've completed this migration to and fro for over fifty years.

Once Neil is scheduled to back his semi into our loading chute, Pete calls Daren Clever, our brand inspector and friend whom we see with the cycles of the season. Daren wears comfortable western mule shoes and carries a pink livestock cane when he comes to our place to inspect our shipment of calves. He once said he used the pink cane just because he could. Pete's comfortable with Daren. I think they speak the same language about the minds of horses and their own. The conversation rolls quickly into roping horses and plans for summer training.

Brand inspectors like Daren are important fixtures in the animal industry. Part law enforcers, part gatekeepers, they inspect each animal before it's transported and the ownership is officially transferred. When Daren checks each brand at our ranch, the cattle move across the corral while his eyes search for the correct brand as though he'd turned on a personal x-ray. After he certifies what he saw and writes up the paperwork on the hood of his white truck, he and Pete talk about who bought what roping horse from whom and how they plan to winter over.

Two character brands, like ours, the Spear Quarter Circle and Two Quarter Circle, reach back to an earlier time. The tradition of branding animals to claim ownership goes back thousands of years to the Chinese who branded their farm animals. The Greeks, unimaginably, branded their slaves. In the American West, large herds of cattle grazed vast open ranges. When gathered in the fall for market, the ranchers needed a method to identify their own cattle. So in the spring round-ups, all the calves were branded. Hot branding irons waited in open fires to claim each one. The brand might be an initial, or if two men had the same initial, it became an initial with a bar or wings or a running symbol. Brands are registered for county recording purposes and today can be researched in state brand books. As the West grew and cattle herds increased, ranchers ran out of unique two character brands and a third character was added. Here, a long-time ranch to the south used the S Bar S brand for five generations.

Once a practical necessity, a brand today is often elevated to a sign of a special connection to the past, to a fraternal bond with the ideals of America's West. A number of developments in our county claim both a name and a brand. For example, the Storm Mountain Ranch development's brand is a running river over an image of a mountain range. Alpine Mountain Ranch's brand is the letter "A" without the cross bar over the letter "M" all enclosed in a circle. Neither development raises cattle nor has a need for a brand, but I recently noticed a woman in the produce section of the grocery store with the name of her home development and brand embroidered on her canvas handbag. Perhaps hers served as a kind of New West coat of arms?

John Clayton in *Writers on the Range* believes we should be thankful for those who clamor for a connection to the history of the American West, just as this woman in the produce section, for it is they who help keep the memory and traditions alive. Where the newcomers and old-timers meet, there's opportunity for "a vibrant culture." I hope it's so. I hope those who wear their brands on their ball caps and handbags come to know the long history of branding possessions and the true role branding plays in the cattle industry. And I hope where ego meets true history, the energy of the ego will turn to devoted advocate, a new loyal westerner. What a rich meeting there would be between Daren, our brand inspector with his pink staff, and the woman whose home in the Alpine Development was once also home to cattle Daren inspected years ago, before they were loaded onto a semi headed to market for the last time.

Summer

Lilies and Rhubarb

The Mark Norman homestead cabin

Chapter Seven

Lilies and Rhubarb

The clouds cleared yesterday afternoon, and a blue Colorado sky emerged. Some of the pregnant mares and new foals slept in the warm sunshine, relieved, the spring deluge over. I, too, sat in my favorite soft chair on the deck, soaking in the sunny warmth while I wished my mother "Happy Mother's Day," the clear skies like fresh laundry, the first page of a book, or the day after forgiveness.

Summer 2005

Yellow and delicately arched, the glacial lilies come into bloom first on the nearby hillside. I think to myself that the gods painted a picture of "sweet" and put it by the roadside. Each year the lilies take me back to other spring times.

Before my daughter, Cassidy, went to school, we rode the ATV to the bend in the road to see the lilies in early spring. The little hillside was just big enough for a preschooler to walk around without getting discouraged. The lilies bloomed across the crown of the hill, interspersed with the deep periwinkle and pink spring beauties about four inches high, and white snowdrops, little minions, just barely above the ground. In that wild spring nursery, we found lily petals as delicate as Cassidy's young skin and clusters of periwinkle blossoms on stems as hardy as Cassidy's little legs. It was our first secret ritual of delight in the springtime.

Come early June, we headed out again into the hillsides, hopping on the four-wheeler, scissors and plastic bags in the toolbox, and Cass hanging on tightly behind me. This time our destination was an old homestead I had discovered while running in the hills years earlier. Its abandoned garden still had rhubarb plants that emerged faithfully each year. At the bend in the road we headed north onto eight hundred acres of land we leased for grazing.

On the way, we passed the old Norman homestead. Tom Komfala, an electrician from Gallup, New Mexico, owned the place. His Uncle Estefen, an immigrant from Austria, originally purchased the place in 1931 from Burt Norman, son of Mark Norman, a homesteader from Bedfordshire, England. Tom and his son, Steve, lived there June through October and improved the place every year, maybe a new fence line, a fresh road grading, or a repair project on some of their equipment. In the fall, they hunted and invited old friends to join them.

Many part-time residents, like Tom, who live in our rural areas, love their land; they govern, tidy, and nurture their new-found homesteads. Some understand rural living better than others. Those who do, take responsibility for learning how to live on the land. They know in Colorado a landowner must "fence out" livestock. They know weed management not only affects their meadows but the neighbor's. They know water is shared with other water rights owners, and come summer there's a delicate dance between neighbors to move river water through the hay meadows and down through one's horse pastures.

The land Tom nurtures doesn't provide a living or set his table, but those who came before him needed a home and a livelihood. Their dreams were of opportunity and self sufficiency, home and family, and of a land their hands could draw over and transform. So it was for the Normans who settled on the place in 1896 and from whom Tom's uncle later purchased the land and homestead.

Widower, Mark Norman, raised three sons and five daughters there. They used to ride to school two miles on horseback across a creek in Dutch Gulch, named after the Dutchman, Winkleman. One spring afternoon, the four youngest daughters were coming home from school on horseback, two girls to a horse. Facing the high running creek, the horse Edith, the youngest daughter, and Grace, the older daughter were riding stopped at the creek to drink. Its front feet sunk in the mud and as it attempted to jump forward it fell in the water. Grace scrambled to the bank but Edith floated down the creek. The girls ran to get their father who was working nearby. They found her quickly in the creek with a hoof print on her forehead. She had most likely been kicked by the horse as it scrambled to right itself. I listened as Mary Mosher, a daughter of one of the remaining Norman sisters, told this story to Cassidy, me, and our 4-H group one afternoon—only that day she left out the part about her mother's sister, Edith, being killed.

Mary married Mike Mosher, the son of the land owner next to the Norman homestead. Once married, Mike and Mary bought land across the river and settled down to raise three daughters. Tragically, two of Mary and Mike's daughters died in adulthood echoing the loss suffered by Mary's mother and her grandfather.

One of those daughters left a granddaughter behind and Mary watched over her knowing that, although the child lived with her father, she needed a mother like the meadows need rain in June. At the end of the summer, it was Mary who came to her granddaughter's 4-H sewing demonstration. She brought a camera in a purple velvet Royal Crown bag trimmed in gold. As Cassidy and I sat next to her at dinner, I asked kiddingly, "Mary, what are you doing with a bag of booze at a 4-H ceremony?" She just smiled and laughed a bit self-consciously. "It was the best thing I could find to carry my camera in. I guess I'll keep everyone guessing, won't I?"

I always think of Mary when I travel past her family's place. She persevered through loss and heartbreak in her life and quietly carried a purple bag trimmed in gold so she could help make happy memories for a granddaughter whose mother had left her behind.

Once past Mary's grandparents' homestead, now Tom's place, Cass and I rode through the rugged hay ground to an old summer homestead. Abandoned in the forties, the only visible remnant of the place is an old car, which continues to sink deeper into the landscape each June. Although overgrown with sage and tall grasses, we could still make out what used to be the family garden. No longer surrounded in fence, but with a few old posts scattered on the ground, the only hint of what used to be a fifty-by-fifty foot garden, were ten or so rhubarb plants. The plants, obviously hardy, weren't nearly as big as they once were, but they continue to produce enough tender stalks of rhubarb to make our annual adventure to harvest worthwhile.

We each took take a pair of scissors and clipped the light cherry-red stalks, sometimes searching a bit to find the plants hiding behind the sage brush. I watched Cassidy comfortable in a pioneer's garden and I felt new again, as though the energy and vitality of her youth were mine. When the plastic grocery bags were full, we headed down through old grazing areas fed by the creek in Dutchman's Gulch.

Once home, we made stewed rhubarb to serve with our granola and planned a rhubarb cobbler for dessert one night. The rest we cut into pieces to freeze for later in the summer.

Just as the homestead seemed to be slipping away each spring, sinking farther into the landscape, the trips to the glacial lilies, the pioneer's garden, and my little preschooler slipped away, too. Cassidy said yesterday afternoon she had dinner with her boyfriend's parents in Casper, Wyoming, during a weekend of college rodeo. And then over the phone last week she explained how she would fit in extra classes when she went to graduate school next year.

Come spring I usually don't hop on the four-wheeler to go up on the crowned hillside covered in lilies, pink beauties, and white snowdrops anymore. I know I won't hear from beside me, "Mommy, look how many there are! And look I found some more little blue ones with the pink inside. Can we pick some and take them home?"

I haven't been back to the homestead, either, to see if there's any rhubarb to harvest in the old garden. The land is owned by someone else now. Cassidy and I only talk about it when we tell friends or visitors what it used to be like when we were younger.

"Yeah, it was cool. My mom and I would go all the way up into...What's that place called Mom?"

"You know, the old summer homestead."

"Yeah, the homestead. We rode the four-wheeler to this old place and picked rhubarb, bags of rhubarb."

And then without missing a beat, she'd ask, "Mom, when are we gonna have stewed rhubarb again? We never have it anymore."

Those moments came and slipped away as quickly as days of carpooling and laundry and homework turned into days of quiet dinners for two and a new puppy curled up on the couch between my husband and me. I enjoy the freedom of my days, but I miss Cassidy's *joie de vivre,* the world through her eyes in spring, and her warm soft cheek against mine as we sit quietly by the fire.

If Mary were here, I believe she would tell me to find a purple velvet Royal Crown bag with gold trim and put my camera in it. Then she'd say, "Be ready with that camera. There will be more precious moments." In doing so, I believe Mary answered the same call the lilies, pink beauties, and white snowdrops answer every spring as well as the call the pioneers answered when they planted rhubarb in the soil of their homestead, not knowing if they would have rhubarb cobbler in June.

Summer

Mighty

Cassidy rounding the third barrel and heading home

Chapter Eight

Mighty

Colorado blue skies emerged by morning light. The pregnant mares slept, soothed by sunshine, awaiting the arrival of their little ones. Observing their slumber, I decided anticipating foaling according to a date seems only a numerical estimation fully dependent on the rhythms of the natural world.

Summer 2005

We were all worried about Mighty, the last mare to foal. The last few days she acted as though she was ready to labor: lie down, kick a leg, switch her tail, and stand up and go on grazing. Then last night, when she lay down, she moved as though she wanted to get up, but then rocked back and forth several times. A few minutes later, she was visiting along the fence line with the other mares.

Around the breakfast table, Cassidy, Pete, and I had asked each other, "Is Mighty just trying to get the foal out, so she won't be poisoned? Was the baby too big, backwards, or otherwise dead?" I'd seen a stillborn calf before. I helped Pete pull it from its mother in the birthing stall. Just as we pulled the leg hard enough to get the length of the baby from its mother's womb, the leg ripped from its body, and we sat in old blood and toxic waste. The stench wafted for hours over the barn and seeped into the house.

Hoping I wouldn't see that again, I nevertheless walked briskly to the barn after breakfast, carrying the anxiety of someone inadvertently first to the scene of a car accident. Guarded, I entered the mare barn, holding my breath. I knew it would be a good sign if I saw Mighty standing, but I didn't. Cautiously I took a few more steps and spotted her mane covered with sawdust, and as I looked at her belly, I imagined it still full, weighted, and lumbering beneath her. But with a few steps more, close to the bars on the stall, I looked down, and saw, finally, a foal trying mightily to stand up.

The little colt's presence in the stall was as beautiful as his red roan coloring and straight legs. Between eating her sweet grain and licking her new little one, Mighty looked as though her baby arrived just as nature's wisdom intended. She looked liked a mother who'd given birth many times before, enjoying her meal, the results of her labor rightfully beside her. I could almost hear her saying in between sweet grasps of hay, "Mary, please, I've done this before. I know what I'm doing. You all worry too much. Trust me next time. Isn't he beautiful? Could you get me a little more water before you go?"

I noticed Mighty hadn't cleaned yet (the birthing sac and the placenta hadn't been pushed out from her womb), but if all went well, they would in two to four hours. As she nudged and licked her baby, she accomplished two important biological miracles. First, she stimulated his nervous system, then while the foal nursed, the same hormone released in a human mother, oxytocin, encourages her womb to contract and release the birthing sac and placenta, completing the birthing cycle.

Pete and I would be checking on Mighty and her new little baby throughout the day, filled with a relief that comes from renewed faith in nature's ways. I suppose too we'd feel as though we were good stewards, adequate midwives; that our relationship was both accountable and trustworthy not unlike the feelings we had as new parents.

Mighty represents a racing blood line within the quarter horse breed. The foal's sire, "Designer Red," is a quarter horse stud bred for the kind of speed needed for barrel horse racing. Mighty is "double bred" to Jet Deck blood, meaning both her sire and dam come from the same bloodlines. And "Jet Deck" bloodlines come from "Easy Jet," who had what many believe to be the most controversial and successful racing career of any American Quarter Horse.

The American Quarter Horse breed evolved from the Foundation American Quarter Horse, which included Arab, Turk, and Barb bloodlines and the bloodlines brought to colonial America from England and Ireland in the early 1600s. The result was a heavily muscled animal capable of satisfying the colonist's love of short-distance racing.

This Foundation Quarter Horse moved west with the pioneers and played a vital role in the development of the West. Known for their "cow sense," that ability to understand the movements of cows and respond effectively to them and a steady disposition, the quarter horse was tailored for the demands of settling and surviving in the western wilderness.

From the late nineteenth century until the mid-twentieth century, the Foundation Quarter Horse remained a fine athlete and westerners' companion. Then in 1940, the first breed native to the United States was officially established as the American

Quarter Horse. Bloodlines from Routt County Quarter Horse breeders were a part of the foundation of America's first native breed. Names like Quentin Semotan, Evelyn Peavey Semotan, Marshall Peavy, Coke Roberds, and Si Dawson all played a role in the development of Quarter Horses, influencing breeding programs throughout the rest of the country.

Quentin Semotan once lived just across the road. He raised cattle, horses, and four daughters. Jo Semotan, his youngest daughter, lives just west of here on the ranch where her parents retired in 1969. In 1946 Quentin purchased Starduster, one of those foundation quarter horses. As Quentin took his registered Herefords to show, he also took Starduster to livestock shows in Denver, Chicago, California, Fort Worth, and beyond, winning Grand Champion at the National Western Stock Show and Champion of Champions at the Southwest Exposition Fat Stock Show in Fort Worth. Starduster became a pre-eminent grandsire of AQHA Champions during his lifetime.

Starduster left the valley at thirteen in a trade of dollars down and a Two Bars colt to Ralph Bell in California and later to Thane Lancaster in Idaho where Starduster continued breeding mares until his death at thirty-one. Although he's been gone over fifty years from this valley, the Starduster's line and Quentin's fine eye for horses continues to pass through our own breeding program. From a gray gelding called Smokey out of the Starduster line, to a two-year-old gelding waiting for training, and our own stallion, Dudley, who goes back to Starduster, Quentin's spirit remains nearby.

In more than fifty years, the breed has been made even more versatile. Bloodlines within the breed have been developed for modern-day re-creations of the activities and work of the Old West cowboys in cutting, cowhorse, and reining competitions, traditional rodeo roping and barrel racing competitions, and the English riding competitions of dressage and jumping.

And for Mighty's little red roan, when he's older, he will one day run a clover leaf pattern of the barrel race. When Cassidy's home from school, she'll nurture and teach the little colt how to trust, how to move, and how to run on home after the third barrel. This will bring a sense of satisfaction she and others don't find when they purchase an already trained horse. For oftentimes in purchasing a horse, the horse's history is diffuse, the truth about its nature blurred. Purchasing a horse that someone else has developed and trained somehow also feels as though you've cheated, you haven't done the work; you just stepped into the stirrup and all the recognition rightfully belonged to someone else.

So in the next few years, Cassidy will swing her leg over the saddle on the red roan and know she belongs there. The two of them will run down the arena, around that first barrel, across the arena to the second, on to the third barrel at the far end before heading for home, knowing they did it themselves. She will know the feeling of the good steward, of the trustworthy teacher and guardian. Cassidy will know what Quentin and other horseman and horsewomen have always known: the relationship between man and animal nurtures both, requiring a certain mutual dependence and trust, ultimately priceless, the affiliation and bond irreplaceable.

Summer

A Robin's Nest

The author and her daughter, Cassidy

Chapter Nine

A Robin's Nest

The aspen leaves rustle in the cool wind. The leaves of the hostas, tomato plants, and pink climbing roses droop heavily with rain, just as heavily as our sleep at midnight after the tympanis thundered and lightning bolted from the heavens to earth over and over again.

Summer 2005

I usually make a hundred beelines to the shed everyday in the spring and summer when the garden beds need to be tilled and sorted through. I'm in and out grabbing my favorite shovel, hoe, and pruning shears. I unburden the shed of multiple garden hoses in order to dig in to the back corner where an old wooden nail cask stands. There I reclaim numerous decorative garden stakes like the smiling sun, the milk cow, and the singing cowgirl. Once a bed is carefully cleaned of last fall's leaves and lightly tilled, I plant a stake to announce that my gardening season has begun. In the frenzy of the early garden season, little did I know what I missed scurrying through my garden chores.

Last year we'd found a perfect nest tucked away in a corner of one of the horse trailers. Cassidy, not wanting to throw it away, brought it back to the house and put it on top of the electric box on the back wall of the garage. The dished out creation of dead grasses, twigs, and dry mud was too hard to toss out without taking time to admire the artistry of a bird's

home. After our first look of appreciation and amaze-
ment at nature's architecture, we didn't give it much
thought. It seemed a relic and of no future use to anyone or any bird. Like a cherished souvenir from Paris,
tucked away in a shoebox, we'd simply forgotten
about it.

Then that day in June, out of the corner of my
eye, I thought I saw movement above the electric box
as I passed by. I looked back, but all I saw was an
empty nest. Returning again to the shed, I looked
carefully, stopping a good distance from the nest.
Within seconds, there it was, a dark pointed beak and
then another, until I saw three baby robins peeking
out of their adoptive home. I was surprised to see the
nest being used. Although somewhat protected, nestled against the garage, it was certainly nearby
human coming and going, which seemed simply
against a bird's natural drive for survival.

Later that afternoon, the mother robin startled
me by leaping abruptly from the nest and flying to
the aspens beyond. Of course I knew she hoped I'd follow her attempt to distract me from her brood. I felt
bad. I wanted to assure her I meant no harm. I didn't
want to add to her anxiety. I wondered how she and I
would accomplish our seasonal tasks: hers, mothering; mine, gardening. But we carried on, she and I,
the next two weeks or so. Even though I made my
approach farther away, she still swooshed out of the
nest as I came by and scolded me from the aspens. I
tried to take as few trips to the shed as I could by
gathering as many things as I needed each time. But
she still swooshed and squawked at me whenever I
came near.

It didn't seem to take long for the brood to fill out
the nest. Both mother and father robin help feed
them: at first regurgitated sustenance is brought to

the nest, and then it's the real thing — larvae and earthworms. About the time it looked as though they'd outgrown the nest, they were gone. I'd never seen them take a practice flight or wander through the grass looking for bugs or worms. I wondered if a predator had taken them all. I thought our cat, the most lethal of bird predators, was the most likely villain, perhaps nabbing the poor fledglings as they found their way through the grass practicing their beak dive for earthworms. But we have other predators too, like owls and hawks and snakes.

I hoped though, that they'd made their way out of the nest on winged flight, safely landing on an aspen or cottonwood branch, following after their father who feeds and cares for them up to two weeks after they fledge or leave the nest. As he care takes the little ones, the mother robin can begin her second clutch of the season. If she needs to build another nest, it may take her up to six days to complete it. If not, she freshens up the old nest with new blades of grass within a few days.

~ ~ ~ ~

Now semi-conscious on a lazy Saturday morning in August, I remember Cassidy's white truck is gone: her parking space, empty. She returned to school yesterday. Andy's on the road again headed for another rodeo in Wyoming. Slowly, I feel as though someone picked up my favorite book and turned the page without my permission. Overnight the laundry room emptied out, the ironing board's no longer a piece of furniture in the dining room, and Cassidy's bare bedroom waits to become a retreat again for guests.

After the school year had settled in, Pete and I found ourselves sitting in silence over steaming bowls of chili. Slowly, we buttered our crackers and blew on the chili until it cooled off enough to eat. After a couple of bites, he looked up and said, "I can't believe how quiet it is when no one's here."

I looked into the living room and saw the emptiness in dim evening light. I thought, "Wow, we've been doing this for a few years, and we still haven't made friends with the silence."

In a small voice, Pete said, "Maybe we just need a puppy."

I knew all summer I wouldn't want Cassidy's short summer stay to end. After the push and pull of adolescence, Cassidy and I were beginning to find our way in friendship. In the kitchen over the summer and waiting for breakfast, she would stand next to me at the stove and put her arm around me. With a youthful sing song in her voice, she'd ask, "Hey, what ya doin' Mom? Can I help?" I smiled inside and thought, "It's nice to have you next to me again in the kitchen."

Part of me loves the freedom of having dinner when I want and not when sports schedules and homework demand it. I love not listening for the front door to open and close at midnight. I love no longer being a network spy on the phone with another parent sharing clandestine information about the next party in the woods.

But I miss watching horse shows, rodeos, and high school sports with friends and parents. The prom committee doesn't call me to help set up. And Cassidy's crew doesn't come around anymore: the children who grew up beside her and knew her better than we did before they left home.

While the silences may feel too long in the evening, I find some comfort in the ease of staying in touch by cell phone, briefly tethered through waves of satellite magic I still cannot comprehend.

Our conversations are often brief and business like. She'll call and say, "Hey Mom, tell Dad I found a used truck grill guard for sale. A kid from Montrose has it, and he can bring it to the rodeo in Laramie next week. It's a good price. I think he's asking $400."

Cassidy needed a truck grill guard to protect her and her truck if she ever ran into a deer or elk on the road while driving. In this part of the country the guard is an important piece of safety equipment and an asking price of $400 is considerably less than a retail price of $1,200.

Sometimes they're simple announcements, like, "Hi Mom, I just got out of my test. It was so hard. But I think I did OK."

Other calls, particularly in the evening, are slower and more reflective. "Mom, I'm not sure if I should go to the Career Fair next week. I may want to go to graduate school, and I'm not sure I want to try and work in sales for a company like Purina."

"You know, Cass, no matter what you do, it would be a good experience just to go through a few interviews."

"I know, Mom, but I got a lot of other things I have to do this week, and I don't know if I want to take the time."

"Well, think about it. You never know what might come out of talking to people in the business."

We often don't come to conclusions in the magic of those satellite waves, but after we say, "Love ya," her internal debate will have form.

Although the mother and father robins' natural cycles are transitory and brief, Pete and I continue to act as the father robin, who takes his fledglings into the wider world of the aspens and cottonwoods—his purpose to provide that little bit of reassurance as they step out into their new life. Unlike the father robin that stays with his brood for only two weeks or so, we continue supporting our children's transition from fledgling to young adults over a number of years. Surely the nearness of our voices on a cell phone will nurture their survival.

With the shift in responsibilities as a parent, however, I find myself in search of a renewed sense of purpose. The drive to nurture my children was so strong that I understand why the mother robin nested in less than a perfect world, when nature's instinct compelled her to begin her first clutch of the season and then rebuild for the second clutch. The mother robin will continue her reproductive cycle throughout her lifespan, her purpose in life clear. For me, I have fulfilled the dream of creating a family and the days ahead offer an opportunity to find other ways to create meaning and fulfillment in everyday life.

Reflecting on forging a new sense of purpose in mid-life, I'm reminded of Victor Frankl, a Viennese psychiatrist, who survived the Holocaust. Frankl recognized that animals have instincts to guide them. For humans in traditional societies, however, instincts are replaced with social traditions. Out of his suffering in the concentration camps, Frankl developed the theory that man found meaning in life through experiencing love and commitment to others by involvement in creative endeavors, such as music, art, building, writing, and invention, and in practicing compassion, bravery, and humor. Frankl's words settle over me.

Struggling one day with letting go of all the days of active parenting, I looked at Frankl's notes on my desk and then put them away in my research notebook. I turned off my computer and drove north about fifteen minutes to see a close friend who lives at the

Boot Jack Ranch. One of the trails that led into the Hahn's Peak area came through Boot Jack over a century ago. My friend, Barb Ross, and her husband, Jim, live in a small cabin where she grows the finest gourmet lettuces I've ever tasted.

Over tea, our conversations have a way of making our lives visible to each other and to ourselves: simple words powerful enough to clarify, reassure, and free. I told her about the robin's nest story and how I recognize my drive to mother in the robin's instinctual drive to nest. "I'm realizing it's difficult to leave day to day mothering behind. It's hard to imagine another focus as fulfilling and meaningful, but I know I need to move on in my life."

Before I finished, Barb rose from her chair, walked to her bookcase, and pulled a notebook from a drawer. The sections were marked several times over. I saw sticky notes in layers sticking out of the side of the notebook and another round out the top, marking pages not to be forgotten.

"I remembered this quote about a nest. You've got to have it," she claimed. "Here it is." She turned to look at me and explained, "A friend gave this to me as a note inside a real nest as a gift and I've never seen it again."

The Nest

I was a home, a sanctuary, a place to rest and nest the tiny carriers of seeds and possibilities which have broken open and flow out on their own. Now I have been abandoned, of necessity, so the next of the cycle can emerge. If you try to hold on to me past my time I will crumble in your hands because nothing can be permanent. All must change form in nature. It is time to release your dreams in faith, to the world at large, and return. (Dawn Markova's *I Will Not Die An Unlived Life,* [Conari Press, 2000])

As I left Barb and headed home, I found reassurance in Markova's words. Just as the mother robin's second clutch leaves the nest and her cycle is complete, I too will set myself free to imagine a new landscape. And as Frankl suggested, I will let love, creativity, and compassion be my guide. Like a potter forming the pot as the wheel spins beneath, my hands will form a new landscape in which to live, one in which the past is relinquished, yet informs the path I take and the imprint of my steps.

As I do, I will take comfort in knowing that somewhere the mother robin will go on digging up earthworms and sleeping in aspen and cottonwoods. As the light of day slips away, she will fly south, only to return when spring beckons her to tidy yet another nest. I will gather ripened tomatoes and Yukon Gold potatoes for dinner. Another September of color will warm us, and we'll stack old cottonwood to warm the kitchen on cool autumn mornings. She and I will steadfastly continue the call to life, whether driven by instinct or by the drive to create a meaningful life in community.

Summer

My Little Vaquero

Andy and Cream Puff

Chapter Ten

My Little Vaquero

It's June, and the dry thirsty west welcomes, yearns for damp, soaking rains like grandparents welcome grandchildren: arms open and hearts waiting to be filled and sated.

Summer 2005

The picture in my hand shows a blond-headed little boy wearing a gray suede vest, red checkered cowboy shirt, gray suede chaps, and his favorite straw hat. I remember how the red checkered cotton polyester cloth felt in my hands as I pushed it through my sewing machine: so light, the pieces so small.

The little buckaroo sits astride a palomino Welsh pony under a soft summer sky. Andy's little boots, scuffed and well worn, served primarily as the home for his spurs. He loved to hear them jingle and jangle as he walked, just like his dad's. I remember as I poised the camera, arranging the shot so both Andy and his new Welsh pony, Cream Puff, could fill the whole picture, Andy, waved back at me, as if to say, "It's me, Andy. I'm a cowboy."

That was before my little cowboy went for a ride with his dad in our meadow early that summer on Cream Puff. At four, Andy's legs just barely reached to the middle of Cream Puff's belly. But he'd been riding stick horses since he could run and hop around the living room, and in his mind, that qualified him for just about any steed he might saddle up.

Pete and Andy wandered toward the far side of the property, guiding their horses around pocket gopher holes, so the horses wouldn't stumble; and of course, Andy was checking out his spurs, and in his best cowboy voice hollering, "Giddy up."

The adjacent property line belonged to a long-time ranching family. They no longer raised dairy cows or Herefords, but a son-in-law raised Corrientes, a longhorn breed of cattle from Mexico used for steer roping. Naturally there was a bull on the place, and he looked just like a mount you might see in a Mexican restaurant: horns spanning the wall above the bar, and his eyes following you all the way to your table.

Neither the bull nor the neighbors believed in fences. So the Corriente bull frequently came visiting, the door always open. Just about the time my cowboys got comfortable in their saddles, the neighboring bull easily charged through a down section of fence believing some playmates had come to play.

I'd just put Cassidy down in the sun on her blanket on the living room floor. As I stood up, I looked out the picture window and realized Andy and Cream Puff were galloping full speed down the road toward the house, Andy frozen in his saddle. A few seconds later, Pete's horse followed clumsily, the saddle loose and sagging off to the right, and Pete vanishing from the small swell of hillside above.

I ran out of the house as Andy screamed, "Mom, get me off, get me off!" I put my hands firmly under his arms, swung him out of his saddle, and placed him gently on the ground. With tears trailing down his cheeks and in deep sobbing breaths he reported, "Cream Puff wouldn't stop! Cream Puff wouldn't stop!" When he no longer gasped for air I ask, "Andy, where's your dad?"

It came out that Pete's two-year-old colt startled and in a fit of panic, bucked wildly, pitching Pete to the ground. Cream Puff felt the colt's same terror, spun around, and stampeded for home. Andy grabbed the saddle horn; the once boisterous cowboy hanging on for all he was worth.

About that time, I saw Pete walking down the road, his shirt untucked, hair disheveled, and holding his right arm. Although Pete's arm hurt, he perhaps felt more the sting of a father's failure to protect his young son, as well as a cowboy's defeat, one in which the command of his horse was lost when the Corriente charged.

Andy never saddled up again that summer. What would happen to the vest and chaps, the red checkered shirt, the spurs that jingled and jangled? Would they be forever lost in the horror of a loose Corriente bull?

In the traumatic afternoon, Pete and Andy had faced what the earliest settlers discovered when they migrated to the ranges of the Rio Grande and farther west to California. Raising cattle as a small enterprise to supplement their farming in the northeast, they managed docile livestock on foot with the help of a cow dog. Once American settlers began settling in the South and West, where open ranges meant large herds of roaming cattle, they easily assumed these animals, too, would be docile. However, the first time a settler faced a wild Spanish bull, thinking of his docile herd back home, he probably bolted just like Cream Puff and Andy. They soon learned the Spanish cattle were dangerous and had to be approached not only on horseback, but by those who knew how to handle this new wild breed of cattle.

If he were to ever be a real cowboy, Andy would have to learn what the Mexican *vaqueros,* the true ancestors of the American cowboy, taught the set-tlers. The *vaqueros* rode the ranges of the south-western United States in the eighteenth century, moving cattle from Mexico north to New Mexico and west to California. After centuries of managing large herds, the *vaqueros* taught the settlers how to round up the herd, brand, and move them long distances. The *vaquero* tradition of roping livestock with a *reata,* a braided rawhide lariat, continues today, a century and a half later, and their philosophy of horse train-ing: beginning colts with an eye towards patience and a natural bitting progression, from the snaffle bit, the hackamore, to the two-reined horse and finally the bridled horse, are highly valued by trainers who truly understand physical and emotional maturation of the horse.

During those years we didn't know if Andy would ever ask about working with the mind of a horse or ask about the swing of a *reata.* He would wear baggy pants, a do rag on his head, and practice his break dancing in the commons of the middle school before we would hear his spurs jingle and jangle again. But he continued watching his father care for his horses, saddle up, and ride in the arena and in nearby hillsides. I suppose Andy never got so far away from seeing some of himself in his father. The summer he turned ten, he agreed to attend a week-long 4-H horse camp by himself, where he could test himself in both the unfamiliar territory of being away from home and an oddly anxious and famil-iar territory of horses.

Back home again, we realized the trendy break dancer had reunited with that young cowboy in the gray suede vest and the red checkered cowboy shirt. He signed up for a 4-H horse project and shopped for western shirts, Wranglers, and cowboy boots. By the time he was sixteen, he traded in horse shows for team roping and saddle bronc schools. He teamed up with his roping partner, Jess Franz, whose grandfather, Pat Tellier, hauled the boys to ropings on weekends. He pleaded for us to sign the waiver on the application for a saddle bronco school in eastern Colorado run by a National Finals Rodeo cowboy. "Please, Dad, sign my waiver. Saddle bronc riding is the safest livestock event. It's the real thing; it's the classic cowboy event." After an initial, "no," Pete and I acquiesced. We felt as though, if done correctly, it was a relatively safe sport for Andy.

A new chapter was underway, a transformation, hard won I imagine, of a young boy facing and taming his fears; an adolescent reaching for an identity; and a young man mining and claiming his own relationship, not only with his father but with an animal that would eventually lead him to his own sense of personal competence.

We were never sure why California had crept inside Andy when he imagined himself in college, but California Polytechnic University was his first choice. The University offered both an International Agricultural Business program and a rodeo team. The mix suited Andy. After a year and a half of school however, Andy took time off to, perhaps inevitably, head to Texas where the cultural fabric is woven with cowboys and horses, spurs, and wild rags (silk scarves), pickups and live-in trailers. He always dreamed and anticipated an interlude from school, and there, in Stephenville, where more cowboys live than any other place in the West, he found a horse trainer who hired interns: able-bodied young men, who managed the physical demands of keeping and training horses, all in exchange for learning the art and business of shaping the mind and body of a horse.

The schedule was demanding: up at 6 A.M. and in bed at 9 P.M. The interns mucked out stalls, warmed up horses, kept the tack organized and ready to go, and then worked on their own colts and their own skills. Not a day off for four months. I saw Andy following in the same footsteps of the old-time cowboys, hiring onto a large spread or trail-driving outfit, looking for a place, looking for themselves in the landscape.

Craig, the trainer, saw a certain way Andy had with young horses: the quiet approach, the patient manner, and the desire to know more about the mind of a horse. The training from Craig harked back to the horsemanship training the *vaqueros* shared with the settlers. Craig believed that horse training was a partnership, not a relationship of dominance. Andy understood this. "Craig would kill us if he ever saw us yanking on a horse's mouth." A trainer was to use his mind and understanding to build a partnership with the horse.

Andy left Texas that year, returned to school, and graduated two years later. Little did we know then that he would find his way back to Texas so quickly to answer the same call many *vaqueros* and American cowboys did after the round-ups of the eighteenth and nineteenth centuries, and work his way into the world of professional rodeo cowboys.

With the branding done and a long season of work behind them, the cowboys challenged one another in what they called a "rodeo" from the Spanish word *rodear* or round-up. Hundreds of *vaqueros* from neighboring ranches, who worked herds in the tens of thousands, competed in games of skill based on horsemanship. Events included a variety of races, the riding of wild horses or broncs and roping events necessitating great skill with a lariat. The rodeos were dangerous, requiring a cowboy to be a skilled horseman. The entertainment of the *rodear* lives on today in professional rodeo and other western riding sports.

Unlike mothers of the 19th century cowboys, I get a call while Andy's on the road of the PRCA rodeo circuit. I'm anxious to hear from him. When he rides the rodeo trail, I never know for sure where he is, if he got where he was going, or if he walked away after riding his last bronc. In the evenings when he rides, I check my watch, and when I think his ride is over, I settle into the couch and think about other things, knowing or at least assuming all is well in the world: Andy rode, dusted off his hat if need be, and walked away from another wild horse.

Tonight the caller ID says California. He still has his phone number from school. On the other end I hear, "Hey, Mom, you won't believe it. I won the 'Biggest Little Rodeo in Texas.' I beat out some of the big boys, Mom, like Tom Reeves," his bronc riding teacher. "Yeah, I've been intimidated by these guys all month because they're the pros, but today I just concentrated on my ride, and I had a good hopper of a horse." He scored an eighty-two, his best ever score. "The judge told me I had a 'great spurrin' ride. And the clown, an ex-WWF, World Wrestling Federation, guy with a long pony tail, came up to me after the ride and said, 'You're the man; you're the man.'"

Like a young settler riding side by side with the *vaqueros,* Andy is earning his way each time he finds his way to a small Texas town, saddles up, and hops on his next bronc. And while his father and I feel certain wonder in watching a young man search for himself, we will always cherish that photo of a little boy atop Cream Puff, in a gray suede vest and red checkered shirt. For in his wave to the camera and his unspoken words, "It's me, Andy. I'm a cowboy," he seemed to know what direction he would one day travel.

Summer

Gifts of the Harvest

Raking hay

Chapter Eleven

Gifts of the Harvest

Sunrise bathes the potted lavenders, dianthus pinks, deep purple pansies, curly parsley, and passionate red geraniums. A posy imbues the morning, and I am a child again, sitting quietly in a pew listening to "Praise God from Whom All Blessings Flow."

Summer 2005

As summer tips from its peak, hay season arrives. Haying in ranch country is a team effort: hands are needed to cut, rake, and bale. Today, I join the haying team to rake the meadows Pete's already cut. Sitting in the tractor I wait for his directions. As he stands in the cab door of our 6300 John Deere, above the noise of the diesel engine he yells, "Run it at 1800 or 2,000 and just keep going until you're done."

I nod my head and he steps down off the tractor. I shut the door and turn on the radio, making sure I've tuned in NPR before I engage the clutch and the PTO, the power take-off drive that runs the rake. I'll be driving down and around the hay meadow most of the afternoon, raking rows of dry, soft-colored hay Pete cut three days ago. My job is to run the tractor at optimum RPMs, miss the irrigation ditches and the fence lines, push one row one way, turn around and push the next row up against the first one, and then start all over again.

I'm lucky today. The air conditioner in the John Deere is working. I don't have to leave the door open to get a breeze through the cab. Without it, the heat from an August sun mixed with the heat rising off the engine suffocates, challenging one's endurance, even as the marvel of machinery does all the work.

Over the years we've hayed eighty to 150 acres, yielding 150 to 300 tons of hay, depending on the year. The cold in May, the moisture in June, and the rain in August control hay season. Man may believe he's conquered and managed the natural world, but ranchers know it's not true. Ranchers, as close as they work to the natural world, know they only have control over how they respond to Mother Earth's winds, rains, dry spells, freezes, floods, and pests. She acts, and ranchers must accept and understand the relationship in order to reply.

Our crop this summer is one of our best. Pete fertilized in the spring. The rains came in June and didn't freeze, giving the grass a good start. Then through July, Pete irrigated the meadows with a quiet precision and pride. The hay will feed our small group of Red Angus cattle through the winter—most often from November to late April.

I enjoy making order in the John Deere. I don't worry about the list in my day timer, although raking is on my "to do" list. And in order to make order, I must stay with the monotony; I must stay with the meditation, or I won't stay in the cab long enough to complete my work. Raking forces an unusual kind of western meditation, similar to all meditation: sometimes comforting, sometimes disquieting.

After I round up all the loose grass, Pete will drive right over the rows as the round baler inhales the dry grass hay with the help of ingenious sensors, electrical connections, pulleys, rubber belts, hydraulics, and steel arms. As he drives, the baler tells him to make small adjustments so the bale is built equally. He steers to the right a bit and then to the left, keeping track of the arrows on the screen. When the baler's full, a beeper tells him to stop, to allow the baler to make a final wrap with baling twine, and then it tells him to push the three quarters of a ton loaf of meadow grass out of the baler. It rolls a few feet and gently rocks back and forth before coming to rest. Each bale reminds me of one of my hot canning jars pulled out of the canner and placed on the counter: the true harvest of the season ready for the still and short days ahead.

Girls and women are known for their ability to rake up a meadow with a tidiness men don't often master. I want to demonstrate this every year so I concentrate on the wheel of the tractor, making sure it rolls just to the side of the row I'm raking up, so I won't miss any stray strands of hay. When I find it hard to concentrate, I figure how much longer it will be until "All Things Considered" is broadcast. When it comes on, I know I can rake for several more hours because my mind will easily go back and forth between RPMs and news from NPR.

I know I can raise the rake, turn a full 180 degrees, and start back up the next row, gently letting the rake down as I hear the market report or an interview from Afghanistan or Baghdad. While I make clear-cut paths across a meadow, I'm on Wall Street and then in a Burka sitting in a classroom for girls, celebrating their freedom to learn. I try to imagine Rwandan children left parentless by civil war and young girls sold into sex trade slavery around the world. It all seems so far away. I find myself still in the cab of the John Deere, the diesel engine running with a steadiness John Deeres are known for. My imagination is incapable of stretching far enough to know how abandoned children sleep at night or how those young girls ever come to know themselves as anything other than a commodity, something to recycle, something to throw away once it's past its prime.

Back and forth across the meadow I go, turning grass into long rows of order, into a world that makes sense. Around five o'clock, I stop the tractor, turn off the PTO, lower the rake and the front bucket. Stepping out of the cab, I feel like I did when I took off my roller skates after skating up and down the sidewalks of my childhood neighborhood: my feet, stationary, bracing the ride all afternoon, now slowly take each step into the stubby grass, testing for blood and life with each step.

Turning to head east across the meadows, I look across "my field," the one I pulled together, organized, and set in civilized windrows. I feel peaceful as I look at the outcome of my labor. Just a few minutes away, I'll walk in the front door, shake off my shoes, and fill a glass with iced tea.

I feel guilty: to work outside and wander home through open fields; to work outside and never fear civil war, imprisonment, my daughter barred from a classroom, or Al Qaeda hiding out nearby while I sleep. I hold what I hear in one hand, and the meditation and solitude of turning meadow grass into neat windrows in the other. In doing so, I see and feel even more clearly the gift of running the John Deere at 2,000 RPMs in the heat of an August afternoon.

Summer

My Grandfather's Footsteps

Axel C. Mortensen, early 1920s

Chapter Twelve

My Grandfather's Footsteps

As summer drew near, I discovered heritage tomato plants from Siberia, Greenland, and Nova Scotia at the nursery: the ultimate in hardiness for northern gardening zones. Instinctively, I sensed their value to all who might pass by and knew if I didn't grasp them, I would never see them again. It was the same instinct nudging me to linger with my newborn; the same instinct waking me to the winter of my mother's life.

Summer 2005

When my mother reminisces about her childhood, she always calls her birthplace "the farm." Her mother, Mabel, grew up there, near Brayton, Iowa. Mabel's father, Owen Fowler Ide, purchased that farm from his adoptive parents. Owen preferred reading *Cicero* and participating in state politics to farming, and for twenty years raised horses, chickens, dairy cows, corn, and hay on six forty-acre sections for twenty years. He called the farm Spring View for its fine spring water.

In 1917, a Danish immigrant, Axel Mortensen, traveled by the Spring View Farm looking for work. Owen hired Axel, a hardy and handsome man, just shy of five foot nine and weighing 180 pounds. His square dimpled jaw line and blond hair suggested a certain competence for life. Axel, who one day would become my grandfather, traveled a great distance before coming to the Spring View Farm. In 1912, he sailed on the *Empress of Ireland* to Quebec, and from there he traveled by train alone to Exira, Iowa, to join his brother. He found a succession of jobs, first as a farm laborer and then making barn doors for fifteen cents an hour. During the harvest seasons of 1916 and 1917, he worked in the wheat fields of North Dakota before riding the rails back to Iowa in 1917, when he took Owen up on his offer to work on the farm.

It was there he fell in love with my grandmother. Their courtship survived my grandfather's service in WW I, upon which he returned to Brayton and married her in 1919. Owen offered the newly-weds an opportunity to stay on and share in the life on the Spring View Farm, and so they did. A year later, my grandmother gave birth to my mother, the first of their five children.

Eager though Mabel and Axel were to succeed on the farm, for three years they faced the waxing and waning of a poor livestock market, blackleg (a disease found in poultry), and two weather disasters: crop-damaging hailstorms and drought. Surely, this tested not only their optimism and ability to persevere, but their very identity.

In an effort to remain on the farm, Axel purchased a local cream station, gathering cream from local dairies and shipping it to Omaha. He also sold mineral supplements for cattle long before it was standard practice. Unfortunately, although both enterprises creatively used local resources and markets, within a year, both failed to provide enough financial support for his family.

My grandfather must have lain awake at night, so far from the gentle hills of Aalborg, Denmark, stirring with a kind of primal anxiety, a fear of physical survival itself. Enduring the unmeasured losses of both parents, his homeland, a life on the farm, and the failures of his personal enterprises, life demanded from him a will to breathe, to live, to survive. So, just as he had done since he disembarked from the *Empress of Ireland,* he gathered himself and, with the help of his wife, resourcefully found employment in Chicago with the United States Postal Service.

~~~

Thirty years later, as a child visiting my grandparents in Cheyenne, I found the only remnants of my grandparents' agricultural roots in a small garden in their backyard. My grandfather raised delicious green peas, lettuce, corn, carrots, and potatoes. His green thumb even extended over the fence facing the alley. Every year he tended sweet peas and hollyhocks that grew with the help of chicken wire on the backyard fence. They flowered into the alley each summer. My grandmother loved what she called, "Axel's Hollyhock Lane."

In the summer of 1979, with the coming of our first child and our move to the country-side of the Elk River Valley, I stepped into the soil of my own garden reminiscent of my grandfather welcoming his first child while working on the Springview Farm in 1920. Pete and I embraced a romantic vision of a sustainable agrarian aspect to our life and then watched it prove ephemeral the first harvest season. The earth, in all its potential, had its own rhythm and temperament.

With only the help of *The Almanac of Rural Living,* I naively thought I could raise all our vegetables. So I marked out a 30'x20' garden with raised beds and complementary planting, so the right plants lived together and flourished. I thrilled at the sight of my new ambitious garden filled with potatoes, peas, beans, broccoli, cabbage, cauliflower, and corn. Whether I was watering or watching the garden grow, my heart slowed and my mind rested as I felt tethered to the rhythms of soil at work during the height of its season.

In August of that first year though, I discovered that corn doesn't grow at 7,000 feet in a growing season of at best eighty days. I learned that inside my beautiful broccoli and cauliflower, weevils had multiplied exponentially. As I checked my old time recipe of sauerkraut in its crock, faith in my ability to put up food for my family evaporated when mold grew on the surface. My potatoes thrived, but some turned green. The extension agent informed me that potatoes exposed to the sun develop a poisonous toxin. Of course, my family survived without my toil in the garden; the grocery store saved me from my failures as a provider.

Through a modest window of my own garden failures, I could identify the disappointment my grandfather must have felt when he couldn't sustain a life for his family on the farm. What sense of failure he must have overcome to carry on and find a way to make a life for his family, even if it meant leaving a place he had finally called home. He responded the only way he could, by adjusting to life's mutable pulse.

Once in Chicago, my grandfather adjusted to urban life. He took the 'L,' Chicago's early rapid transit system, to the train station and worked on the postal trains traveling both east and west and north and south across the mid-section of an expanding nation. He rented a small apartment in downtown Chicago near schools and parks. Renting out one of the rooms allowed him to supplement his simple wage enough to support the family. With pleasure and relief, he summoned them to Chicago in April of 1925.

After five years of stable employment and a growing family, now two girls and two boys, Axel and Mabel felt the draw of the open spaces of the West in which to raise their children. Axel applied for a transfer with the United States Postal Service to Cheyenne, Wyoming, where he was hired in 1930.

Even though Jefferson's ideal agrarian society never came to be, remnants of its spirit remain and seem to be embodied in the appeal of the West, its myths and its realities. Men and women, like my grandparents, who came west found a rebirth in their new life. Cowboys found new identities on the ranges of Texas. Homesteaders found the independence and self-sufficiency they dreamed of, sometimes surviving the hardships of new land, poor weather, and cyclical agricultural economies, and sometimes not. To them, Jefferson's words described their yearning for a spirit nourished by open landscapes and independence.

When my grandfather moved his family from Chicago to Cheyenne, Wyoming, he wasn't' looking for land but a better way of life for his family and opportunities for his growing children. An immigrant, he had continued to move on each time the opportunity to better his life arose. Once settled in Cheyenne on Duff Avenue however, he never left until his death. The West had finally offered him what he had been looking for: independence, self-sufficiency, open spaces for his children, and an accessible and growing community in which to support his family.

The Springview Farm and the hope it once held for my grandmother and grandfather became a distant memory during those years in Cheyenne. However, when my mother visits our ranch every year at fair time in August, she brings that memory back to life as though she's once again a child on the farm.

During a recent visit, with the irrigation water flowing peacefully near us, my mother and I picked raspberries in my garden. In a quiet reverie, she began, "Oh, the water in the ditch reminds me so much of being home on the farm. You know, I spent summers helping my grandmother wash dishes after every meal. She insisted on using every plate she had to feed the hay crew. I remember taking out fresh pies and lemonade to the crew in the middle of the afternoon. Those summer days were so hot in Iowa. I'll never forget watching my grandfather late in the evening at the kitchen table. The big meal was served at noon, so at night he'd just pour himself a tall glass of ice tea sweetened with lots of sugar, really just thick with sugar. He'd spread two slices of homemade bread with lots of fresh butter and then carefully lay just the thinnest slices of onion you ever saw on top of the bread. It must have tasted so fresh and cool to him. I can't imagine how he kept going those days. The work was so hard."

My mother and I continued to pick the ripe berries as the late morning sun seeped through the aspen leaves onto my raspberry patch, eating a few and then carefully collecting the harvest in odd-sized strainers. I see in my mother a little girl at home in a summer kitchen on the screened-in porch of her grandparents' home. I imagine a little girl wandering freely between her parents' house and the main farmhouse where her grandparents lived.

When my mother and I had captured as many ripe raspberries as we could find, my mother turned and said quietly to me, "I really can't imagine why anyone would want to be anywhere else."

Whether she and I were standing on the soil of her memories of the Springview Farm or the mulch surrounding my raspberry bushes, with water flowing peacefully nearby, we were standing for that moment in the footprints of a man who had made his own path: from Denmark, to Iowa, to Chicago, and finally out West to Cheyenne, Wyoming. Looking back, I imagine that he, too, at the moment he realized his dream of independence and self-sufficiency in the West, couldn't imagine wanting to be anywhere else.

Fall
Mabe

Mabel Ide Mortensen, Cheyenne, Wyoming, 1985

Chapter Thirteen

Mabe

Cottonwood and aspen leaves line the driveway. Gathered by the wind, they roll up against the meadow grasses, creating a dark brown ruffled edging. It reminds me of an elderly woman who taught me the art of tatting. She lived across the Colorado River near an orchard of sweet Jonathan apples, still small and real in your hand, like the old woman's gift of tying knots with string.

- Fall 2005

As my coffee mug emptied out, I looked across the kitchen at the two grocery bags of Gala apples on my counter. This sleepy Sunday morning challenged my enthusiastic canning goals. Last Friday, I thumbed through my recipe file and picked out recipes for "Spiced Applesauce," "Cranberry Applesauce," and "Chunky Lemon Applesauce." I'd envisioned the canned foods cooling on my counter, popping to seal, staring back at me in red rose, light lemon, and apple spice. Then I savored the thought of each jar tucked away in dark storage, ready to bring down for dinner in January when the winds blow and the snow gathers in soft mounds outside my window. It didn't take long for the dreams to win out over the emptiness in my coffee cup. So I placed my big canning pot on the back burner, gathered and cleaned enough pint and quart jars for the applesauce, and gently poured the bag of Galas into the kitchen sink.

Between quick peeling strokes and selecting the next apple in the pile, memories of canning with my grandmother twenty-five-years ago in our first home—the old dairy barn north of Mad Creek— appeared on the other side of my kitchen window. I can still see the fine deftness with which she peeled pears, her fingers fine-boned, her hands still strong and agile. Peeling the red and green skins away, I remember family stories about women working in the summer kitchen of the old family farmhouse, when the women cooked for the haying crews and canned fruits and vegetables for the days ahead. I find myself envious of the comfort in being with other women, sharing the work, helping one another remember we're not alone. Now I realize, standing with my grandmother all those years ago, peeling and canning those tender pear halves, I felt the same comfort.

My maternal grandmother grew up in west central Iowa near Brayton. The family called her "Mabe," short for her birth name, Mabel. We grandchildren called her "Grandma Mort," short for her married name, "Mortensen." It fit her comfortably, like the pinafore aprons she wore tending the baked ham and light rolls in the oven when I was a child in her small and modest 1930s kitchen. In retrospect, the comfort of that kitchen was perhaps even deeper than her name, for there we found her at ease, at rest with herself.

Her mother, Lizzie Cotton, the only child of English immigrants, met Owen Fowler Ide, when she was seventeen years old, near Brayton, Iowa. Owen had suffered and navigated an uneven childhood. His biological parents died when he was quite young; his father died at age seventy, just seven months after Owen's birth, and his mother died prematurely at thirty-five. At three and a half, in 1870, he was taken in and adopted by Harriet and Owen Fowler, his mother's adoptive parents, who were then in their seventies. Eventually, because of their failing health, thought perhaps to be from tuberculosis, Owen was sent to live in Brayton, Iowa, in 1880 and adopted by friends of the family, Oliver and Emily Jane Smith. His new adoptive mother was a teacher from New York, and she and Oliver were resolute in sending Owen to attend high school in Exira, Iowa, and later in Ames, Iowa (Iowa State University). While Owen never faced a childhood on his own or as an orphan in an institutional setting, one can only imagine the emotional difficulties he faced, even though he was faithfully passed from hand to hand, from family to friend, until his adoptive home in Iowa steadied, and family for Owen took root and endured.

Lizzie and Owen raised four children, three daughters and one son, on an Iowa farm. The old farmhouse and barn, painted with "Springview Farm" in white on its upper reaches, are no longer there. But the rolling hills, reminiscent of northern Denmark, still flow like deep gentle ocean waves. Grandma Mort wandered freely there, roaming nearby hills in search of wild flowers in the spring, berry patches in late summer, and crabapples and red haws in the fall. Cornstalks still rise from the earth as they did a hundred years ago, when my grandmother played hide n' seek and make-believe among the rows near her home. The fresh water spring, which still flows, sang to her and cooled her feet. And when, in her early adolescence she suffered from odd seizure-like episodes and was required to stay home from school and rest, she found solace in following the flow of that spring until she tired.

After high school graduation, she began teaching at the Pleasant Ridge School where both her mother and older sister had taught. It was thought at the time the stress of teaching thirty students and the ongoing indoor confinement brought on another bout of seizures. She was referred by the family doctor to a sanitarium in Lincoln, Nebraska, near the home of Williams Jennings Bryan. She reported later in life that there were "crazies" and "some on the verge" with her in the hospital. She spent those summer months of 1917 under observation, playing tennis with one of the male doctors, enjoying lively conversation with a female Irish doctor, and absorbing the nuances of the natural landscape. Later that summer, she underwent minor surgery after which doctors declared her cured. Today, it's believed she suffered from juvenile epilepsy, which subsided as she matured. She never suffered again from these early bouts, nor did she speak often of her experiences at the Fairview Hospital.

Each time I remember this story, I wonder how it was that my great-grandfather entrusted his daughter to the doctors at the sanitarium. Just eight years before my grandmother's stay, Stanley Hall, founder of the American Psychological Association, invited Sigmund Freud to give a series of lectures in America on his ground-breaking concepts of psychoanalysis in his publication *The Interpretation of Dreams*. Perhaps, my great-grandfather had read of Freud and the new science of psychology. Or perhaps, his innate intellectual curiosity and belief in Dr. Koob, the family physician, allowed him to have the faith enough to spend a valuable sum of money on professional help for his Mabe in Lincoln.

Owen Ide had carefully put money away for all his children's educations. But my grandmother's treatment in Lincoln cost one hundred dollars a week for three months – all the money that he saved for her education. So although the opportunity for a college education had been sacrificed, his daughter came home to lead a normal life, teaching school at Pleasant Ridge.

In the early 1980s, my grandmother and grandfather often visited us in the fall as the aspens and cottonwoods turned in the Elk River Valley. One year, when we were ready to slaughter the chickens, my grandmother, at eighty-three, said, "Let's get to those chickens and dress them out. Do you have a blow torch? You'll need a big pot of boiling water and some tweezers. I haven't dressed out a chicken since I lived on the farm, but that's not something you'd forget." She laughed quietly, her eyes twinkling and young.

A photo from that visit shows my grandmother in a creamy floral apron, holding up a chicken with those fine-boned hands, helping Pete burn the pin hairs off the chicken with a blow torch. I see joy in her eyes, and she is, at that moment, the teacher at Pleasant Ridge School, enjoying her pupils as much as she's enjoying the lesson. I wonder where the scars are from that summer of 1917. There's nothing in the picture to suggest she lived with "crazies" at seventeen or that a medical condition, unknown at the time, cost her a coveted college education. In all my conversations with her, I never heard what it felt like to be in a sanitarium. She never told me if neighbors whispered or if her students, whose families may have heard rumors about her medical history, treated her the same when she stood in front of the Pleasant Ridge one-room school.

I knew only that she smiled when she worked, that she spoke of friends and family often and with care, that she told funny stories while she quietly beat everyone at Scrabble, that her cookies were always fresh and layered carefully between wax paper, and that she stayed steady in life through faith.

She offered few windows into her innermost sanctums. The only glimpse I ever had came in a letter she wrote to a family member in which she shared, "Sorrow and heartache must have a part in every life—and they came [to her]. But without them we would never learn to weep with those who weep, or know the comfort of having loving friends weep with us."

That particular September, when the chickens were put in the freezer and jars of brilliant pears in the pantry, my grandparents got in their baby blue Ford Pinto and headed home. My grandfather hugged me as he always did, like a bear. My grandmother hugged me and told me, as she usually did, "Now you take good care of your family. And come see us soon, won't you?"

Throughout my life, I have felt my grandmother's enduring optimism, her unconditional regard. Now I realize that in her embrace, my great-grandfather's arms were also near. He, a man who had known his own parents' abandonment as a child, yet came to understand the importance of steadfastness and unconditional acceptance when he was adopted by Oliver and Emily. He, a man who in his unfailing commitment to his Mabe, showered her with a loving, emotional legacy, which would sustain her and her descendants for a lifetime, linking his spirit to mine and to all whom she so tenderly touched.

Fall
Round-Up

Rounding up steers
From left, Dawn Serafin, Beth Trujillo, and Andy

Chapter Fourteen

Round-Up

*The meadow grass turns brown from the top down.
The sage and oak brush are still green; the choke cher-
ries, ripe. Pete lights the kitchen stove before breakfast
and wears an extra flannel shirt over his work shirt to
stave off the chill. The cottonwoods gave up early and
look motley in sad golds and browns. My gardening
newsletter suggested keeping remay, a protective covering, handy for covering tomatoes and yellow beans.
Some think tomorrow will be the last day of summer.*

- Fall 2005

The roping steers wandered through the front
yard; their rangy bodies and mature horns
looked as if they had just come off the Chisholm Trail.
Several times a season, the group of ten finds a way
out of the corral at the end of the arena, often led by
a ringleader who feels just a bit wilder than the rest.
So this morning I was not surprised. I was sure they
had an itch to get out and wander and graze. They'd
been confined to the corral for the summer season of
team roping, and the urge to be free, to search out
their own food, sent them through a weakness in the
fence—a broken wire, a top rail askew.

Once out, they gladly grazed on a still green
lawn. A quick and successful round-up would take a
bit of planning and good luck. Our understanding of
the way cattle think, whether they be roping steers,
mother cows, calves, or bulls, tells us what pace to

follow and at what angle relative to the animal we need to drive them. The best angle to drive cattle from is approximately forty-five degrees from their tail. If you push too far ahead, they turn back. If you lag behind, they take their own independent track.

Today, we didn't saddle up; the round-up would only be from the front yard down the drive-way, across an open grass area, and into the arena. Pete grabbed the four-wheeler; I helped Andy move them out of the yard while Pete waited at the end of the drive to push them toward the open arena gate. Because they can scatter like fireflies, we were all as ready as we could be should one dart away or try to scale a fence. By the time we finished this morning, they escaped across the road to the neighbor's barnyard and back again. The morning round-up, while less than smooth, ended successfully. The steers settled down in their corral with hay and a full water tank, and in the morning sun, relinquished their rebellion.

Round-ups, referring to the gathering and moving of cattle, can vary in size, from our moving them out of the yard, to trailing large herds to market in days gone by, or moving cattle from summer grazing land back down to winter pastures. The quick round-up of our roping steers reminds me of the traditional fall round-ups that mark a change in the natural agricultural seasons. We usually gather our herd of mother cows off the nearby hillsides late in October. They often do part of our work for us by coming down to the gate just across the road from their wintering grounds as the weather turns. Instinct tells them they need to get back home to survive the coming winter. I often tease Pete, "Hey, you know your ladies are waiting at the gate for you. Aren't they a little early this year? They must be tired of feeding themselves."

Local ranchers do the same, driving their herds from summer pastures near the Continental Divide to their home meadows. The herds may travel quietly along county dirt roads or the main county road busy with local and seasonal hunter traffic. The ranchers may get help from family, friends, or others who love to ride and to trail cattle. Some ranching families here and in other parts of the West advertise cattle drives to those who want to touch the spirit of the Old Chisholm Trail and the cowboys who drove its length late in the nineteenth century. The annual ritual gathers not only the cattle, but those who love the marking of the seasons, the slow walk from the high land to the low land.

These one-day trail drives remain true remnants of the famous trail drives from the wide open ranges of Texas to Dodge City and Abilene. It was on the trail that the American cowboy made his name. The work on the trail in the late 1800s was long and hard. The trail outfits would cover twelve to fifteen miles a day trailing 500-1,500 head at a time. The drive lasted two to three months and posed frequent danger to the cowboys. The herd might spook and stampede through camp. River crossings also posed danger as the swift currents carried off cattle and cowboy alike.

Round-up and trailing traditions in the American West follow in the footsteps of the Mexican *vaqueros,* native cowboys who learned from their predecessors, the Spanish *caballeros* or noble horsemen. The early *caballeros* developed their methods of rounding up livestock from an historical relationship with Spanish knights of the thirteenth century. According to Donald Chavez, in *Cowboys – Vaqueros: Origins of the First American Cowboys,* the *caballeros* first moved and controlled cattle with a loop fashioned out of a rope and attached to the end of a knights' lance. As they approached the cow, they put the loop over the animal's head, and with the help of and coordination with other *caballeros,* "rounded-up" the cow. By the sixteenth century, Mexican *vaqueros* carried on in the *caballeros* tradition by perfecting the lasso technique by using just a *reata,* a long rope, made from braided rawhide, some sixty-feet long. Swinging the reatta at distance was a fine feat. Once the loop of the rope landed and slipped over the head of the cow, they dallied or tied the other end of the rope to the saddle horn.

When we gather our mother cows and bring them back to their wintering feeding ground, pushing them through oak brush, down trails, and along the road to our main meadow, I think what little we've known about our ties to thirteenth-century Spanish knights. While we don't often throw a loop over the head of a cow or steer during a round-up because our horses help drive and gather our cows, the loop of a lariat or rope is a necessary tool at times to control cattle. Whether it's to catch one and treat it for illness or injury in open land or to catch a calf for branding and vaccinations, when Andy and Pete throw a rope, and the loop settles over the head of a steer or cow, they have repeated the lessons of the *vaqueros* of Mexico. The loop they form and throw represents not only a link to the history of ranching traditions, but a link connecting father and son in the present moment for a common purpose. And in the linking, their history is also shaped.

Fall

Making Way for Retreat

Hayshed in autumn

Chapter Fifteen

Making Way for Retreat

The welding generator shimmies and fires as Andy welds pieces and parts of pipe fencing. My washing machine works rhythmically, reminding me of the oil and gas pumps hard at work on the Western Colorado Plateau where I once was a child. The swoosh of the rain bird marks a moderato beat, as if a metronome were setting the pace for the chilly fall morning.

-Fall 2005

There's work to do.

I wake up at 5 A.M., making a list for the day ahead: put roast in the crock pot—I could make it all-American or Italian; go to doctor's appointment mid-morning; make hors d'oeuvres for my ladies group at 6 P.M.; buy perennials at the nursery sale; and clean the kitchen floor, again. It's covered in dirt from cowboy boots, running shoes, and gardening slip-ons. There are bits and pieces of the outdoors: blades of grass, crinkled leaves, and earth itself. And if you look carefully, you'd know someone made cookies and peeled potatoes.

This morning Andy walks in the kitchen in his black-and-gray-checked wool pullover from New Zealand. He's donned an army green wool cap, too.

As I watch him grab a stool, "You look like winter. Must be cold outside."

"Yeah. What is it anyway?"

"The thermometer said forty degrees when I came down this morning. It's supposed to be just in the sixties later today."

Pete overhears our conversation and kiddingly asks Andy, "So what did you find around San Luis Obispo? Any ranches? When do we leave?" Pete and Andy always search for land in more moderate climates, like searching for the Holy Grail.

We repeat this conversation each September when the cool temperatures remind us summer is truly over. And while the middle of the day will warm, the start of the day chills ears, fingers, and feet.

After clearing the deck in the kitchen, sweeping the artifacts of life up off the floor, putting dinner in the crock-pot, and hors d'oeuvres in the refrigerator, I head to town looking for perennials to fill in the gardens.

Each fall I replace plants that have failed in my gardens. At first I thought it was just me: I wasn't smart enough about the needs of plants. Then I thought the growing conditions were more challenging than I had realized. And then a few years ago, I submitted; plants die, and some for no earthly reason. When nature finally brought me to my knees, I realized my gardens would never look like those in the gardening magazines with simultaneous blooms covering the page. No, my gardens would be more like unfinished paintings, never brought to completion.

I park in front of one of our local nurseries where they'd advertised perennials 30 to 40 percent off. I need three fire pokers, three Echinacea, three relatives of the rudibeckia, a sedum ground cover, and woodswort. When I gather them for the attendant to count, only one of mine qualified for the sale collection. But I buy them anyway. What do you do when you need the right plant in the right place for its color, height, texture, and bloom time?

With pleasant autumn weather, the days fill in, and dinner comes late. As I tend to the gardens, Pete eagerly tends to his fall list of ranch chores: new corral posts to put in for the roping arena, sheds to paint, a new culvert to put in, equipment and tractor maintenance, and downed cottonwoods to clear out and add to the burn pile. When cool and blustery autumn weather settles in, the days collapse as the hours pass by, and unfinished chores nag like arthritis. Winter is closing in, shutting the door on man's work outside.

After lunch, Pete and Andy work steadily, cutting and welding recycled three-inch oil pipe and a smaller pipe called "sucker rod," for the horses' runs. Although rusty and well used, it makes the ultimate fence. The thirty-yard open extension from the shed will allow the horses to wander out into the sunshine and down to the ditch for water.

The horse shed's been long in coming. It's picturesque now when you stand in front of it. Pete's pleased with the double doors painted in red and trimmed in white. The bottom half of the door is trimmed out with a cross of trim and reminds me of watching *Mr. Ed* on a black and white television in the basement of my childhood home.

Later, when Andy doesn't need Pete to cut sections of rod, he'll sort through a summer's worth of headstalls and bits, cinches and ropes in the barn, putting everything back in its place, so it's handy next spring. Then he'll ride his big Dun, Chico, to keep him sharp in the roping box. Because he wants to sell Chico, he needs to keep him in tip-top shape, so prospective buyers will be tempted.

Building, cleaning, sorting, polishing, planting, preparing for winter; we'll soon retreat inside and take off seasonal work boots and gardening shoes for the last time. The full days of fall will submit to winter's insistent push for retreat. And we will follow, warming our feet by the fire and entering a world away from the smell and feel of horses' sweat under saddle, meadow grass wrapped in sisal twine, and perennials painting the landscape.

Fall

A Shifting Landscape

The former Warren Ranch

Chapter Sixteen

A Shifting Landscape

Early morning, dark and ephemeral, feels like a warm woolen wrap, protective, assuring. Headlights of a lone commuter slip through the opaque resistance as though faith drives the car. I listen for the bugle of a distant bull elk one more time before first light. Soon the day will set sail and children will step off buses parked in front of open doors; and working men and women will turn on lights and tools. Then foredawn's wrap will gracefully slip over the horizon, rounding the earth once again, dark, ephemeral, and opaque.

Fall 2005

When I was a child, my mother baked bread every week. On bread-making mornings she carefully measured her ingredients including flour, salt, yeast, and Morell lard packaged in a blue box, its cover decorated in white mountaintops. In order to measure the lard, she'd spoon the lard into a clear glass measuring cup filled part way with water. The lard would displace the water, increasing the water level in the cup. When the water hit the top of the measuring cup, my mother scooped out the lard and put it in her large green Pyrex mixing bowl. The yeast dissolved in warm water followed, then the flour, salt, maybe an egg or two, and a good stirring, as she added enough flour to make the dough stiff and ready to knead.

Standing eye level with the measuring cup, I never understood the displacement idea—how and why she knew how much lard she actually scooped out. But when I was in junior high and watched her measure her Morrell lard, I felt tethered to a high line, a line used in the backcountry to secure pack horses for the night. The line to her kitchen kept me steady as friends hopped in and out of the circle I'd traveled in since kindergarten. The circle got bigger, but I found myself no longer with my old friends. Pushed back, I stood near the edge. When I watched my mother bake bread, I found refuge from my teenage uncertainties.

I realize my experience of finding comfort in the aroma of my mother's kitchen was not unlike my children finding comfort in their rural lifestyle. As they faced the challenges of negotiating what at times seemed an impossible task—the world of friends, pressures from popular culture, and expectations from others—they found security in the rituals and traditions of the agricultural community and seasons.

As my children and many other 4-H friends went through high school, the dominant culture was not a rural one, even though there was a time when more students did come from ranching families. During the fifties and sixties, the school boasted successive years of wrestling championships at a time when many young men worked hard during hay season and helped with chores on their parents' place. It was not unusual for a student to be a 4-H member wearing Wranglers and cowboy boots and driving a pickup to school.

Participating in our 4-H club as an adult leader, I watched a number of 4-H students negotiate this layered struggle of identity. Several transferred to a school with closer ties to the agricultural community, a school which offered an active Future Farmers of America program in the south of our county where the dominant culture was rural.

Other students, including our own, gradually gained strength and pride in their rural roots and attachment to their way of life. They were able to straddle the divide between a contemporary, fast-paced peer culture and their emerging identities as western citizens, cowboys and cowgirls. They played on the soccer team and also showed pigs at Fair. They skied on the high school ski team and served on the county 4-H Council. They lived in two worlds, but claimed their western sense of self as an enduring identity: their feet rooted in their relationships to animals; their arms wrapped around open lands made up of meadows and hillsides; and interdependence found with families in the rural neighborhood.

Naturally, we've also watched the parents of these children, the ranchers and farmers, face change, too. In our county and in much of the West today, ranching is quickly being transformed from a commercial enterprise conducted by individuals and/or families, to a lifestyle purchased by those who can afford to purchase land at values many times the historical agricultural valuation.

In turn, the ranchers and ranching families leave or sell off their land, and the character of the communities changes to reflect those who make up more and more of the new West. The dominant culture shifts from ranching families to new residents eager to adopt long- standing ideals of the West, such as ownership of private property and individual rights to use that land as one sees fit. The process of gentrification of our rural lands across the country is often pushing out those most intimate with the natural landscape. And in its wake, the warp and weave of rural communities changes, breaks up, breaks apart.

Pete and I recently watched this shift, this changing of hands of the rural landscape. Just down the road, I pass the Warren Ranch on my way to town. Del Sherrod, long-time rancher who grew up on the lower Elk, managed the ranch. He put other ranchers to shame with his work ethic. He fed earlier, fixed fence sooner, and put up hay faster than anyone else in the valley. I don't know if he really ever took Sunday off. His wife, Lynne, was instrumental in developing the Colorado Cattlemen's Land Trust, another entity working toward conservation and protection of rural lands. She commuted to Denver during the week and often traveled around the state to speak passionately for the protection of agricultural lands.

The ranch Del managed was owned by the same family for twenty-seven years. Forest and Ruth Warren owned and lived on the ranch while their adult children ran the family's trucking business in Nebraska. The ranch encompasses 1,600 acres on both sides of the road. To the south, the beautiful and productive hay meadows flow to the river. On the north side, the scrub oak hillsides provide pasture for two hundred steers every summer. An iconic red barn sits right on the road, and the main house stands just across the barnyard, painted a practical brown. A tall wooden windmill turns right off the south-facing deck, the north side of the house protected by several pine trees, honeysuckles, and old-growth lilacs.

After the death of Forest and Ruth, their estate was settled, and the ranch was sold to two local buyers. With assistance from Purchase of Development

Rights (PDR) funds and funds from our state lottery organization, GOCO, the ranch was purchased with a conservation easement. The conservation easement essentially guaranteed the ranch would remain open land in perpetuity. At the time, we were pleased that a local man had taken such an interest in keeping the ranch a working ranch and that the priceless meadows would remain so forever.

The Elk River Valley has had a long history of conservation easements, dating back to the early 1990s when Jay Fetcher, his family, and local land owner, Steve Stranahan, began the conservation easement movement in the Elk River Valley with the help of the American Farmland Trust. Slowly, one by one, ranch owners, including the Warren Ranch's owners, were invited to join in the protection of our beloved neighborhood. Because of their visionary efforts, we all, whether passersby, residents, or newcomers, will always draw nourishment from the inspiring sight of this open ranchland.

Although Del, the long-time ranch manager, stayed on for awhile, he realized change was inevitable and began sorting out his options. He and his wife eventually found a place of their own to improve and ranch in another county. While pleased with their new status as land owners, the displacement they suffered came with loss: loss of the land they had long nurtured and a life-long membership in the local community and family ties.

Much to our surprise, in 2005 the local man and his partner put the Warren ranch up for sale again. We felt betrayed. Had the two men in their promise to be conservators of the land, not made a promise to settle in the neighborhood? The "For Sale" sign didn't stay up long. Had it sold, or had the owner suddenly changed his mind? Not long after, in early 2006, the sale was confirmed. It was under contract to a man from Chicago for eight million dollars.

The world I trusted is changing. I'm wary, and I'm guarded in my old neighborhood just as I was in my old junior high, separated from the world I'd known before I left childhood behind. Each time ranch land is sold to a buyer who can afford to pay development prices, we watch and wait, hoping the buyer will care about it like the ranchers before him. Sometimes buyers do. And we feel as though we know something about the new neighbor's heart. Sometimes buyers don't. And we feel an inflated presence in the home built there, fearing the new owner may never reach out to know the neighborhood he now calls home.

Though disappointed and fearful of what would become of the Warren place, we were heartened to think that by purchasing a property under a conservation easement, the Chicagoan demonstrated his interest in being a good steward. His dedication to the traditions of western ranching was clear both in his commitment to the conservation easement and in his leasing the ranch to a capable local young couple who will carry on raising a family, cattle, and a fine crop of hay.

Driving by the old Warren Ranch, I realize the landscape will remain a backdrop for a traditional rural lifestyle, at least for now. A tie to the land will be preserved through an interdependent relationship between the ranch manager and the ranch. I know too, that the tie to the land will be deepened if the new owner chooses to step out onto his land to learn the art of fixing fence in the spring; to know the satisfaction of checking in on the mother cows and their offspring; to know the joy of walking in verdant meadows as the sun sets; to understand the nuances of setting an irrigation damn; or to warm his feet by the fire after a winter's feeding. For it will be there, in the walking and the doing, in the sensing and the learning, that the owner will truly know his good fortune.

Just as adolescent cultures will always change who's in and who's out, western culture and communities will face change as rural lands are gentrified. In accepting this reality, I hope those new to our community will awaken to the need for both historic and land preservation. I also hope they will awaken to the need for preservation of community: the need to find a way to tie us together—past and present; old timers and newcomers. Just as I was sustained by the comforting ritual of my mother baking bread, I know the development of neighborhood and communal ritual connections will be essential for the sustainability of rural neighborhoods and communities. For if we fail to nurture those community ties and let the warp and weave of our communities break apart, what will sustain us?

Fall

Emma

Emma and Bob

Chapter Seventeen

Emma

Emma, my new Boston Terrier puppy, sleeps in my lap: soft, sweet, like a child. The look of sweetness belies the rambunctious Emma of this morning, biting my bare feet and leaping off the kitchen bench as if she were super dog, her red cape catching the wind.

Fall 2005

In early October, I walked into the Northwest Airline cargo office at the DIA Airport. It reminded me of a tire shop I visited with my father on Saturday mornings as a child: a man's world, no plants, no candy dishes, just an efficient office tracking the comings and goings of the world in motion. I waited for a few minutes as I watched two men working in the large storage area next to the office. Just as I began to wonder who would help me, another man in a Northwest work uniform came through the door and said with a quiet smile, "This must be yours."

The small crate was covered in tape holding in place a package list, breeding papers, and food; arrows pointing up said, "Live Animal" and "Denver" in large letters. Inside, curled up behind a mound of shredded white paper was Emma, a black and white Boston Terrier puppy I'd laid claim to eight weeks ago from a breeder in South Dakota.

Emma's arrival was long awaited. Pete and I had discussed puppies for a couple of years after our children left home. We continued our work at befriending the silence of a childless home, and even though we'd found other points of focus and attention and new patterns of socializing with others, an insistent desire to nurture and to enjoy a trusty canine companion lingered. With questions and discussions about a puppy more frequent, I began searching for the perfect canine.

I knew I wanted a smaller companion dog, but a dog sturdy enough to run, snowshoe, as well as escape the horses headed into the corral or the tractor rounding the corner at the edge of the barn, if need be. And I had always liked my son's dog, Brute, a Boston Terrier who fit well with his life at school: loyal, easy going, and small enough for one-room living. When Brute arrived from the South Dakota breeder, Andy fell in love and so did everyone else. Brute's small, smashed nose, black and white color with a touch of brindle (a lighter brown variation in color subtly streaking through the coat), and apparent sweet disposition earned him unlimited time in laps around the living room of Andy's fraternity house.

Fortunately in late summer, the same South Dakota breeder had a new litter waiting to be weaned from their mother. I searched the faces on the breeder's website and spotted Emma right away: her petite feminine face and striking markings, to me, irresistible. Now, nearly in my possession, I happily greeted her as she peeked out from the airline crate in the Northwest freight terminal.

"If you'll sign here and here, she'll be yours," said the Northwest cargo employee. "She's sure a little bit of a thing." I took a quiet deep breath as I picked her up rested her comfortably in my hands. In a moment of timelessness, I was back again with my children reading, "Goodnight room. Goodnight moon. Goodnight cow jumping over the moon...." And then, just as quickly, I took Emma outside to stretch her spindly legs and take care of business, and then put her in the front seat, nestled in a polar fleece blanket.

Headed back west on the interstate to the ranch, I realized Emma, like so many travelers to new lands, had left behind all she knew: the warmth of family in Mt. Vernon, South Dakota, the smells of their farm, and familiarity of wiggly litter mates. Just as I hoped my children's memories of home would soothe them when the world feels unsettled and unsure, I hoped Emma's sense of being warmly socialized by her family, the comfort of her litter mates, and her mother's breath wash over her as she sleeps on the way to her new home.

Intent on being a good parent to Emma, I read the wisdom of dog training experts on raising puppies. All agreed: crate training was a must for a well-adjusted dog. It felt akin to those childrearing experts, who, twenty-five years ago, said infants should not be placed in the parent's bed. It was essential they grow to understand that they were separate: individual and independent.

I didn't like the advice as a young mother. But Pete and I followed the wisdom of the experts most nights because we wanted to be good parents. We managed nurturing our children as newborns and infants by placing their crib in the room with us: separate and independent, but close and within reach. But some nights, when one of them couldn't sleep or wasn't feeling well, we followed our own intuition and expert advice: we tucked them in between us and slowly their fitfulness or unease receded.

I managed in the same way with Emma. At home I put Emma's crate right next to my bed. Andy had assured me that the enclosed space recreates the den of a dog's forebears and a sense of safety from the outside world. "Mom, don't worry about Emma sleeping through the night. Just put your hand in front of the crate and let her smell you. That's all she needs to know you're there." It worked. After the lights were out, I offered her my fingers through the wire door and she sniffed, licking them a couple times just to make sure, and then she curled up and quietly slept until daylight.

The next morning, I stepped outside with Emma for an early morning walk. From the stair landing, I spotted the hard frost on the lawn. I'm never ready for the cold when it drops in. I know it will warm up during the day, but fall hardens me like a new little transplant for the deep winter ahead. Reluctantly, I began to believe its warning as I awakened to the brisk and the cool.

Emma, too, looked as though she didn't expect the nip. She took a few steps and looked at me for direction. I walked around the corner of the house and Emma padded to keep up, lifting her paws quickly from the biting frost covering the still green grass. She clearly sought a tether to guide and secure her in the face of a small initiation to her new home and the coming harshness of winter on the ranch.

As I watched Emma toddle around the edge of the gardens and sniff the entrance to the garden shed, I felt a subtle apprehension rise. Dogs had come in and out of my house all my married life, but I'd never been in charge, I'd never actually raised my own. Pete, Andy, and Cassidy had, at one time or another, picked out and raised a Border Collie, a Border Collie-Australian Shepherd cross, three Australian shepherds, one St. Bernard, one Border Terrier, a Golden Retriever, and a Boston Terrier—most all of them good ranch dogs. But now, I was the one facing the challenges of actually raising and training a dog.

I continued the same exploration into understanding Emma as I had in understanding my newborn and young children. I read about how dogs think, what motivates them, and what discourages them. I read about when to sign up for obedience classes and about the importance of balance, nurturing her and setting boundaries with her. In my search, I found that many of the answers to the questions had comforting similarities to parenting.

She would need leadership and structure. "I love you, but you can't run into the street after the car. I will understand that you need a place of your own sometimes, like your dog bed, but I'll also know you like to sit near me at night. And when I leave the house, I will turn on the TV to let you know you're not alone and promise you that I'll always come back."

Emma and I returned to the kitchen that first morning, and she fell into her bed by the fire. Here we were, Emma and me, an attentive canine polliwog and her new mother. Ahead of us, we would find comfort in the simple presence of one another just as I found while sitting with Andy or Cassidy while reading their favorite book at bedtime. Ahead of us we would find conflict in differing opinions and misunderstandings, struggles for independence and dependence. But in the work of relationship, the edges around the silence in our home would fade and through the act of befriending Emma, I would find myself enlarged once again by attending to the needs of another being.

Fall

The Days Ahead

CJ Mucklow, CSU Extension Agent

Jay Whaley, 4-H Extension Agent

Chapter Eighteen

The Days Ahead

Wandering out into a brisk morning, my flannel shirt cuts the chilly breeze and my bare legs bristle in protest. I recall August's soothing warmth and the grass I lay in as a child: lush and timeless.

Fall 2005

Every summer, Cassidy trained horses for the county fair. As the third week in August approached, she spent more time in the arena practicing "squaring" her horse up, which meant the horse had to stand evenly on all fours with a stillness that was never easy to perfect. Or she had to ride round and round, working on different riding patterns she might be called upon to perform for the Western Riding class.

Like clockwork, the busy preparation coincided with a turn in the seasons. On the day of the horse show, Cassidy and I would walk out of the house shortly after daybreak with freshly pressed Western shirts, steamed and cleaned cowboy hats, Wranglers, pins, hairspray, and coolers. The chill on my hands and face always felt the same: my eyes teared up and watered, the back of my hands dried out as I walked to the barnyard.

When Cassidy was younger, I feared I would miss something on our list. With the fairgrounds about an hour away, a forgotten bridle or pair of boots would be hard to replace. 4-H members are expected to take care of themselves and their responsibilities as soon as they're able. But as motherhood would have it, it was more difficult for me to wean myself from being helpful. During those years there would be arguments about who was supposed to iron her show shirt or who forgot the "Show Sheen," a fine spray that brightens up a horse's coat.

I struggled to walk the fine line between Cassidy's independence and an appropriate and helpful gesture of support as she made her way through adolescence.

When I couldn't let go, I'd offer reminders. "Cass, don't forget the Western Riding Pattern has two slow circles and only one big circle."

And Cassidy would re-draw the fine line. "Mom, I know, I know. Don't worry about it."

Next time, I'd step back a couple of steps on my journey of letting go and manage, "I think your Western Riding pattern's tough today. I hope Salty picks up the right lead. Good luck."

With the line in place, Cass replies, "Thanks, Mom. Salty was pickin' up his lead yesterday at home. I think he'll be fine."

By the time she was in her final year of high school, however, what Cassidy most needed from me was a perspective, an ear to listen to when the challenges of decision making and responsibility confronted her. Her horse and steer projects were her own entrepreneurial enterprises. She trained, fed, and groomed. She added up the numbers and asked her dad for a final audit and signature. And there she went, into the ring for the last time.

Cassidy and Andy both left for college intent on studying agriculture. Having spent their childhoods on a ranch raising horses, cattle, chickens, pigs, and assorted puppies, and their participation in 4-H the centerpiece of their summers growing up, it wasn't surprising or unusual that both our children went to college seeking a life in agriculture.

Andy graduated from California Polytechnic University with a degree in Agricultural Business with a focus on International Marketing. Cassidy graduated from Colorado State University with a double degree in Agricultural Business and Animal Science. But when they graduated, Pete and I tried to imagine how our children could maintain their ties to agriculture when, by itself, it would never support them. It had been a lifestyle choice for us that shaped their growing up. But the proposition for them seemed a conundrum complicated by the contemporary scale of agricultural economics.

Agricultural operations have existed on the fringes of economic viability since the late 1800s. And while the development of our local resort community has created a healthy economy, one in which young people have the opportunity to find employment outside agriculture, the change in the nature of the community forces many old residents to re-locate or face living at the edge of a re-constructed social milieu.

Searching for answers, I invited our local extension agent, C.J. Mucklow, and our 4-H agent, Jay Whaley, to join me for a cup of coffee at our locals' favorite coffee house to talk about this very challenge facing our children and others of their generation. I was interested in what he thought would be ahead for our children: was there a way to a viable future in agriculture?

The young barista inquired, "What can I get for you?"

C.J. offered, "My treat, what do you want?"

I asked for a cappuccino, and Jay joined in, "I'll have a raspberry latte." He chuckled, "Boy what a sissy drink."

C.J. followed, "I'll have a raspberry latte, too."

"Whipping cream and raspberry syrup too?"

"You bet. Why not? Gotta enjoy life now and then, don't ya?"

Whenever I talked with C.J., I reached up with my eyes to catch his, at well over six feet. He stands easily in his tall frame, his mustache full and his smile joyful. He makes me feel as though I'm just talking to a farmer, sitting on a barrel of peanuts in the old general store.

In the leisure of the moment, as our decadent coffees were prepared, C.J. said, "You wouldn't believe what people want now in their coffee at work. We buy coffee for one another now and then, and the list for the their order just gets longer: soy, organic, shade and hillside grown, whip, no whip, hot, extra hot. You name it. It's crazy."

Jay and I nodded in agreement and joined in the "What happened to all of us?" looks going around in our small conversation.

As we waited, Jay asked, "How's Cassidy doing?"

As a parent, I always appreciated the example he set for the kids in the 4-H program: one of quiet strong leadership and personal responsibility. In turn, he expected those same qualities of the 4-H council, and they responded by growing in his positive, faithful light.

"If you can believe it, she graduates from CSU next month."

"Oh my gosh, how did that happen? What does she want to do?"

"Well, she said to me, 'Yikes, what now, Mom?' and I said, the world's your oyster, sweet pea. It's up to you."

We all laughed, knowing what it was like at twenty-one when we were complaining about school and wanting to be free from it, yet in the same breath realizing just what that meant.

"She may just need to take a year and explore. She's thought about graduate school. She actually took the GREs a couple of weeks ago."

C.J. said, "Oh that's good. I'm glad she did that. She can do anything now." And Jay nodded in agreement. They seemed relieved.

After settling in around the table, I was eager to hear answers to my questions. My reading and research had taken me from the implications of long-term weather predictions for agriculture to urban sprawl, to land preservation, global economics, immigration policy, and loss of rural community ties.

"C.J., I'm really curious about what you think is going to happen to agriculture in the U.S. I know two years ago when we hosted the land stewardship class, you said that the U.S. had to decide whether or not it wanted to raise its own food because it was importing so much. What do you think now?"

"I think there'll always be agriculture in the U.S. It's just a matter of what it's going to look like. The reality of a viable ranch is that it has to be debt free, and the rancher has to have enough cash flow to pay for expenses as he goes: equipment, maintenance, fuel, labor, feed, fertilizer, pesticides, herbicides, and everything else. Because of the economics, it's a big boys' game now."

Then almost as an addendum, C.J. gathered his hands in his lap, scooted up in his chair, and added, "You know Mary, Jay and I almost feel guilty encouraging kids to go into agriculture, because there are so few opportunities now. Like, what do they do? They can manage a ranch for someone who can afford to buy one. They can run a feed store or sell pharmaceuticals. They could work in extension or teach or go to vet school. They could create a niche market for a gourmet food brand or other product from the land. But the reality is that jobs in agriculture, actually on the land, are few and far between."

"Pete and I feel the same way. We almost feel as though we should have told our kids to go into business or marketing or education, but not the School of Agriculture."

With a characteristic quiet in his voice, Jay joined in. "I think our kids chose a lifestyle when they chose to go to School in Agriculture. It was a way of life that they wanted."

I nodded in agreement.

I know our children found relationships and ties in the agricultural community of their childhood that reinforced their own values, ones of friendship, cooperation, and family life. They found a comfort in working with animals and being in the outdoors. Their experiences in the 4-H community pruned and nourished them. They found themselves mirrored in others who valued a similar kind of a life.

After sipping cappuccinos and lattes, all three of us knew these answers to the questions couldn't satisfy. All we could know for certain was that the next generation will more than likely manage the ranches, not own them; they will sell the agricultural products, not necessarily use them. The entrepreneur may develop a value-added agricultural product like organic beef or gourmet cheese; the educator may help us remember where our food comes from; the veterinarian may always care for our animal friends; and perhaps, the policy-minded may enter the arenas of land preservation or international agricultural policy.

Just as I worked at letting go of supporting Cassidy as she journeyed toward independence, I will work at letting go of the unknown, the unanswered question for the future my adult children write for themselves. Whatever the tool, I simply hope they and those with the same desires will make for themselves a place in the world where they will find what Jay believed they were looking for: a way of life that satisfies and sustains.

Winter

The Mailbox

Bill and Cynthia May

Chapter Nineteen

The Mailbox

The sky, light from the moon, rests as clouds seek the east and the moon falls to the west. In a moment morning stirs; a commuter, a crow, a finch, a furnace—the still and the quiet flushed out—as though daybreak, a sled leaving the crest of the hill, the young child pulling in her feet, tightening her grip, leaving the rest to the pull of the earth.

Winter 2005

In twenty-five years, I'd never seen the Mays' wagon wheel mailbox overturned in the barrow pit. But there it was, totaled, by the side of the road. During our winters, the snowplows roll along like defensive linemen tackling a quarterback, with a certain undeniable commitment to the task. A toppled mailbox in winter usually means a new driver behind the wheel who hasn't developed the right touch, a subtle, but exacting pull of the wheel to the right or left. It's as if his brain hasn't yet measured the time and distance correctly.

The mailbox in the barrow pit sadly mirrored the times at the Mays' S Bar S Ranch. In 2004, the family arranged for a realtor to list the ranch and arranged for a ranch auction to sell off old equipment, saddles and tack, household goods, furniture, and a few antiques. Bill and Cynthia May had moved to an assisted-living home in Fruita, Colorado. Bill struggled with Parkinson's for a number of years and recently lost his battle with the disease. Cynthia suffered from a four-wheeler roll-over accident and needed help during her treatment and recovery.

Bill's grandparents, Fred and Anna May, homesteaded on Buck Mountain in North Routt County in the 1901. Then in 1928, they purchased the S Bar S Ranch in 1928 as part of a tax sale. The original ranch consisted of two separate parcels, much of it fertile hay ground, and the rest oak brush hillside, ideal for summer grazing. Bill and Cynthia were second-generation ranchers on the place. They raised four children there: three boys, Jay, David, and Scott, and a girl, Grace.

Cynthia's grandfather, Nat Biffle, rode the trails up through the plains of Texas as a young cowboy with Charles Goodnight, who established early cattle trail driving routes to the northern railheads in the second half of the nineteenth century. They also trailed cattle to Montana and South Dakota selling to Indians along the way. Roots running deep like this in the West make up the bedrock of river bottoms, the foundations of historic barns, and stories told carefully enough to resonate with children born to the twenty-first century.

The Elk River flows around a bend at the Mays' place where the cottonwoods and dogwoods share the banks with woodchucks. In the fall and spring, the bare dogwood branches dazzle commuters as the sun sets through their bare spray, turning the growth to burgundy velvet. Behind the cottonwoods, the homestead house used to stand near numerous sheds and corrals. A couple of older log cabins housed help, and an old hay sled sat near the barn. The ranch now consists of 380 acres of beautiful hay meadow.

Near the Mays' entrance, I once watched a bald eagle sail back and forth above the river, as I waited in my car behind an oversized trailer hauling a newly constructed outhouse for the Forest Service. Others in the car line poked their heads out of their windows and communicated their discovery in sign language to other drivers. The urge to get home dissipated and we forgot about the outhouse as a roadblock. Instead, we dropped our push to get home and relished the freedom and flight of the eagle.

Bill and Cynthia worked hard on their place. It was evident they both shared the love and labor of their place. Therefore, it's not surprising that Cynthia always wore pants. Only once did I see her in a dress. That was for an annual 4-H awards gathering. She looked beautiful in her soft lavender gown. Her work-day wear included men's shirts, roomy pants, and comfortable shoes. I never saw her in a pair of cowboy boots. Contrary to what many believe, wearing cowboy boots doesn't make a rancher or a cowboy. Cynthia went for functional, comfortable shoes while she worked all day on her feet.

Cynthia had other trademarks, too. I could always tell that it was Cynthia who was waving her hand out of the truck to slow the traffic when they drove their cattle down the road. Her hats and bandanas, varying with the seasons, gave her away: wool hats with flaps for winter feeding, sunhats tied under her chin for spring branding, and ball caps for riding the summer range. Cynthia wore bandanas around her neck for warmth in the winter and to absorb the sweat in the summer.

I followed the seasons watching the Mays' mailbox too, Cynthia used to put a wreath on the wagon wheels in December. Sometimes she'd add an old boot or two. On the fourth of July, a flag signaled a certain pride found so often in rural settings. And when the children and grandchildren started getting married on the ranch, a poster board sign was tacked onto the wagon wheels with balloons. The wagon wheel mailbox acted as a message board to the passersby; little reminders of the season and announcements of celebrations to the neighborhood. We knew the S Bar S Ranch was alive, even though it was hard to catch a glimpse of it tucked behind the cottonwoods.

Now the news about the May Ranch was on two large red and white For Sale signs at the entrance to the ranch: "May Ranch for Sale — 380 Acres." The brochure in the newspaper appealed to the imagination of those who longed to be a part of the West: "Here's your opportunity to be a part of a ranching legacy." The asking price: six million dollars. That's just about $15,000 an acre. Not an unusual price for land in this county. However, for a cattleman to make a profit on land priced at $15,000 an acre, he would have to raise more than 1,200 head of cattle on 380 acres. Depending on how the ground was used—part pasture, part hay ground—those 380 acres might sustain fifty head and produce four hundred tons of hay.

Today, however, the real value in the land for the new westerner doesn't necessarily have to be for development. It can be in the protection of the hay meadows through a conservation easement. The conserved and protected open land, stretching from the hillside to the river bank, recently drew in a successful entrepreneur in his thirties. After purchasing the ranch, he improved the river and its banks, built a barn and arena, and created roads and improved fence lines.

As neighbors passed by, we watched intently. While we regretted the leave taking of the May family, we were pleased to know we will always see open meadows just beyond the banks of the Elk. We were pleased this new westerner valued the land for its ability to produce cattle and hay. In the new land owner's commitment to ranching and conservation, our neighborhood will remain familiar.

It's been years since I saw Cynthia walk across County Road 129 to get her mail. It was safer then to walk across the road that takes traffic to north Routt County. Nowadays, more than 2,000 cars a day pass by the May place, most of them commuters, and in the summer, boaters, campers, hikers, and fishermen. I don't see any balloons on the mailbox or a flag on the Fourth of July.

We no longer slow down after branding time when the Mays drove their cattle up to their Forest Service lease ground for summer pasture. These grazing permits, in addition to Bureau of Land Management permits, allow ranchers to utilize public lands for their livestock herds. And we no longer close our front gates when the herd passes by late in the fall on their way back home. Cynthia's note cards of local flowers in watercolor are no longer for sale. We will no longer hear Bill read his cowboy poetry or play his guitar at the Moonhill School House, once a local gathering place for holiday potlucks. And the *Fence Post*, a statewide agricultural publication, no longer publishes Bill's column about the history of his family and ranch operation.

I am encouraged by memories of Bill and Cynthia not to forget how important our traditions, the natural world, and our rural neighborhood are. I will hold onto the importance of celebrating the family and the seasons. I will remember to watch for the bald eagles sailing over the Elk. And I will always hope, that if Bill and Cynthia were still around and they were dragging their mailbox out of the barrow pit with their tractor, those who were passing through the neighborhood and saw the Mays' struggle would understand their need and offer to help.

Winter

Junior

Junior Bedell, 1985

143

Chapter Twenty

Junior

*The foals huddle together in the snow-covered mead-
ows. A winter storm flies in from the west. With long
coats and a quiet mood, they give in to the bleak nip
and chill, joining mother cows, the deer and the elk,
the grosbeaks, and the porcupines in relinquishing the
day to the elements, adopting patience and a certain
stillness necessary for survival.*

Winter 2005

Now in his sixties, he wears a well-seasoned
Carhart jacket, a red plaid shirt with snaps
on the pockets, and Wranglers, probably the same
size he wore in his thirties. His cowboy hat, a well-
used silver belly (a reference to its color) with two
toothpicks tucked in the hat band, sits on his head as
though married to it. I watch Junior walk into one of
the Western stores in town just before Christmas
with hands in his pockets, moving in his own time
zone, not disconnected from the one he's in, just
mindful of his own purpose.

Sitting near the entrance to the store on a cowboy barstool, made out of large old pine, I offer raffle
tickets to Christmas shoppers for our Cattlewomen's
quilt and as soon as Junior's eyes meet mine, he
jumps right in, "So how's Mary? How's the snow out
at your place?"

Weather's always the first point of contact after hello. Once I thought it was silly, superficial, until I heard someone say, "The subject of weather is a safe common denominator. We all experience weather, so it's a place we can meet quickly." And for Junior, me, and other farmers and ranchers, weather is an agricultural heartbeat we hear. We understand its power to create and take away: deep snow pack brings timothy and alfalfa grass to the valley come summer, yet late spring snowstorms endanger newborns.

"Junior, it's climbing the fence posts," I say.

"By God, when we was kids, you couldn't even see the tops of the fence posts. That's the kind of winters we had. I even remember wrapping the legs of our draft horses with burlap so they wouldn't get sores walking through the deep crusty snow. That was a lot of work back then. Sure is great to see ranchers feeding with tractors. But you know if we get snow like this all winter, they may not get out in there far enough to feed. They may spend all their time blowing feed trails. Damn, it's a lotta' work."

Our snow depths are already 30 percent above average, and if you aren't blowing your way out, you're finding it difficult to find a place to put the mother lode of snow. Old timers mark the harshness of the winter, not by statistics, but by the depth of the snow against the fence lines. A "three wire winter" is one in which snow reaches the top wire of the fence. It's then the fence lines, boundaries, demarcations, and broad definitions of the land disappear. Neighbors are no longer separated by barbed wire or fence posts made out of scrub oak, metal, or pine, with the landscape now smooth, rolling, and uninterrupted.

In this deep winter landscape, since the days of silver and gold mining in North Routt, settlers, cowboys, and families have found winter entertainment in cross- country skiing. In Hahn's Peak, once the county seat and 10,000 strong, anyone who was able strapped on a pair of long wooden skis and headed out with a long pole for balance.

Junior's father, Orval Bedell, carried on the wintertime traditions, hiking and skiing surrounding mountain landscapes. He was well known for his winter climbs of Hahn's Peak and Sand Mountain. Junior's father also skied into town one year for the annual ski jumping competition at the Winter Carnival celebration. But before he could leave, Orval had to milk the family's dairy cows. When finished, he and his buddy, Russell Whitmer, cross-country skied into town, a distance of about twenty miles. Junior's dad won the competition and after celebrating his victory, he and Russell strapped on their skis and headed home to milk the cows again.

Junior inherited not only his father's physical sturdiness, but his sense of adventure and hard work, too. In his seventy years in the Elk River Valley and eastern Utah, Junior sheered sheep, shod horses, slept in the cabins of outlaws who ran the Outlaw Trail from Robber's Roost to the Hole in the Wall. He hunted mountain lion for twenty-five years in Western Colorado and eastern Utah and proudly says he "...left footprints where no man, red, black, or white ever walked. You would have to be a mountain lion hunter to understand that." So, when I find myself face to face with him I know the stories await: those of a life of labor, of footprints followed and footprints made, and of people past and present with whom Junior crossed paths.

When the stories begin, they come easily, as Junior is well known for being a jokester. I've learned to watch his eyes and carefully await his punch line, knowing that at any time, I might be taken. And I suppose that's why anyone who knows Junior stops and listens; they know he could strike at any moment, joining the speaker and listener in a brief moment of release from daily life.

So, when I asked him, "Junior, how's your Christmas shopping coming?" I had an idea where our conversation might take us.

"You know, I did pretty darn good with them daughter-in-laws. I got 'em both a broom."

Junior smiles wide and chuckles with pleasure, knowing he might get a rise out of me for suggesting women should just cook and clean. After our laughter, he adds a quiet postscript, "Naw, I got the two of 'em Chamber gift cards. You know they can get what they want." After a deep breath, he settles in his chair with his elbows on the counter, and as though seeing their reflections in the space between us, he says, "I sure like the two of them." Junior seems comforted by their presence, embraced by the widening of family ties.

His oldest son, Chad, won the National Finals Rodeo Steer Wrestling Championship in 1996 and then came back to the Elk River Valley. Chad and his wife, Jen, have made Junior a grandpa twice and when I ask about his latest grandchild, his eyes twinkle and his face softens, "Ya, he's a tiny thing alright. Damn, he's not even big enough yet to hold onto."

Although it's close to Christmas, there's an unusual quiet in the store. The storm from California literally blows sideways down Lincoln Avenue, and the Christmas shoppers who do come in either aren't intimidated by the likes of the weather, or they know the stores will be easier to navigate because no one's out and about.

The slowness makes it easy to listen as Junior tells me he's found a special log hook, called a cant hook, for one of his sons, Travis, who's sawing logs for his own home. The cant hook will work like an old ice hook, allowing one man to move the logs over as he shaves the bark clean. Both his sons, Chad and Travis, came back to the Elk River years ago, continuing both a tie to the land of their extended family and summers of their childhood.

"Well, 'spose I outta get out of here. You tell that husband of yours hello."

Junior stands, tugs at his Wranglers to pull them to his waist, and then turns to look at the back of the store as if the one last present he's looking for is there. He's looking for, but doesn't find, a small rope for a little boy who lives near him in the winter months in eastern Colorado. Junior tells me how cute that kid is when he fools his mom by sneaking out of the kitchen when it's dinner time. I hear Junior's kindness and vulnerability in his obvious enjoyment of the little jokester.

I stand and walk over to the pot of hot cider and pour another cup. Junior grabs a couple of cookies, slips them in his pocket, and begins to walk towards the door. "You take care of Mary, now. Tell that family of yours, Merry Christmas."

Watching Junior walk out the double door, I know I won't see him again until spring. Then one day in April, when I'm out running on the road, he'll come up behind me in his navy blue pickup with his horseshoeing equipment stowed away in the back. He'll slowly come along side me, stop and say, "How's Mary? How's Andy doin'? Is he back from Texas? How'd his winter go? Did he have any luck?"

I know Junior knows what it's like to have a son on the Pro Rodeo Circuit, what it's like when Andy doesn't have any luck, when after each rodeo the phone rings with disappointment. I think Junior is waiting for the luck to change for Andy, for the dream to come true. He's waiting just like he waits for you to take the bait of his story and then belly laughs with you until you're through. In each moment, we're lifted from the firmness of the ground we're standing on, and for that moment, we are in Junior time, suspended from the confinements and structure of daily life, his levity bringing a welcome ease and comfort to our day.

Winter

A Washcloth of Hope

January's Chill

Chapter Twenty-One

A Washcloth of Hope

Now and then I hear a faint howling. I look out to see if a breeze has started up out of the west. The aspen tree that serves as my wind meter is still. I realize the faint crescendo is just the forced air heater pushing a warm breeze into the room, keeping the coolness away. A storm brewing raises the tension in the air like a good drama. I'm disappointed: nothing moving in, nothing moving out. Why is it I find comfort in the stillness, yet listen for change?

Winter 2006

After the Indonesian tsunami, my daughter and I put together "Health Kits" for the survivors. Inside each gallon bag we put a hand towel, a washcloth, a toothbrush, toothpaste, finger nail file, comb, band-aids, and soap. The only part of the survivor's experience with this "Health Kit" that I can imagine is the first time they wash their face and brush their teeth.

I share my struggle out loud with Cassidy, "Can you imagine what it's like to brush your teeth for the first time in days or maybe even weeks? Like after a weekend of trail riding?"

"I can't imagine, Mom."

Then I realized it's so much more. "Can you imagine the whole valley underwater, Cass? Can you imagine what it would be like if we couldn't find each other?"

"Mom, I can't. I just can't imagine anything like that would happen here. It wouldn't, would it?"

I ask myself, "How can we understand what it was like to witness the unimaginable?"

A few nights before Cassidy and I worked on our relief project and just a few short days after the tsunami, the winds whooshed and whirled as I readied for bed. The winds seemed to rage across the valley as though the same force that cracked the earth under the Pacific had come to our part of the world. My husband spoke quietly as we both lay still in bed, "I wonder if the earth is coming to an end?"

While his question was half in jest, we frequently discussed our growing concerns over climatic changes we'd experienced the last several years. We remembered the ash that blew into the house from wildfires three hours away to the west. We remembered the apocalyptic glow of the Zirkel Wilderness burning just over the ridge from our home. And we're all too familiar with the impact of multi-year droughts that threatened our irrigation water three summers ago. We find ourselves, in the drama of the earth, the wind, and the fire, wrestling with a shifting comfort and belief in the earth to a fearful worry that nature's forces may one day have their own way with our beautiful earthly home.

The swing in climate changes varies to a greater extent than ever before. Four years ago we experienced the driest season on record in more than 108 years of record keeping. This year our water shed recorded the second greatest year of snow depth and moisture quantity, while the southwestern part of the state suffered from another year of record low averages for precipitation spawning another year of record-level drought.

The climatic swings and escalating natural disasters continue, and we wondered what it means for us, our children, and our children's children. Should we try to complete our own risk assessment, studying drought reports and predictions, and determine the best place to live under the current patterns of weather change? Or is it just so much bigger than that?

As the Elk River rushes with hope in the spring and then slackens to a shallow whisper come December, I sense both its ability to provide when winter snows are abundant, yet its powerlessness when the winter snows disappoint. I wonder what many of us will face: higher floods, a drought's even tighter stranglehold, wild fires closer to home, grasshoppers and beetles that mutate, dancing through pesticides to the next meal and governmental and public debate over water rights, heated and contentious.

The Indonesians didn't know about risk assessment. The Indonesians didn't even have a tsunami warning system. The earth moved and only the elephants knew to retreat inland to safety. Only the elephants heard the moment the ocean floor shifted and an hour later cried out as the impending tsunami came ashore.

One day, I hope the Indonesians have a tsunami warning system even smarter than the elephants' intuitive powers. Just as I wanted to hope that in the ritual of washing away the soil, a tsunami survivor's resilience is restored, that in one simple act she finds hope, and in one simple act, she lives again. And I wanted to hope that the same kind of deliberate ritual restores our resilience and engenders hope in the face of what appears to be accelerated changes in our climate. Perhaps we'll turn inward, seeking our power to right our carbon footprint in the place we call home. Or we'll draw a cleansing cloth over our daily lives, washing away the excess, breathing in simplicity. Or we'll remember how, when we see a mournful moon or feel a slip of the wind, our mood transforms, and we are entwined, one with the other, and accept the necessity of mending our relationship with all of the natural world.

Winter

In His Father's Workshop

Andy building his pig feeder

Chapter Twenty-Two

In His Father's Workshop

The overcast skies blanket the stars, yet Venus shimmers. Ancient Italians named Venus the goddess of spring and beauty. Romans identified Venus with Aphrodite, the goddess of love and beauty. At nine, I colored Venus purple in my solar system having never been told stories of goddesses, love, and beauty.

Winter 2006

As I stand stirring hot cereal at the stove, Pete checks the automated weather station Andy gave him for Christmas. Before Pete goes out to feed, he always checks it. If the temperature is below twenty degrees, he wears all his heavy insulated canvas clothes: the pants, covered in oil and barb wire tears; his jacket, stained in three different shades—oil, dirt, and manure; his new toasty warm boots, and then his winter gloves and funny warm ranch hat with brown checks and ear flaps pulled down.

When he's all bundled up, feeling like a doughboy, he'll stand in the kitchen with a goofy look on his face and ask me, "Hey, ya' wanna go out on a date?" We both laugh, and I wonder if that makes it easier for him to walk out into the cold, knowing I said yes.

When the weather station reads anything above twenty degrees, Pete travels lightly: jeans, ranch jacket, winter boots, and cap. He doesn't ask for a date on his way out. His step is light and even quickens when the sun lights a blue sky. He takes longer to come back to the house; he might even talk to his brood mares and yearlings. He'll hear news stories from the old radio in the shop while he does a few extra chores.

I guess those degrees let the blood actually move through his body, energizing him. They entice Pete to be at home in the shop, straightening a gate hinge or sorting through tools on the work bench to put them back in their rightful place on the wall. The invitation of a winters morning, where the air is crisp and the sun's rays warm, leads him to enter the cool dark barn and sort through empty feed sacks and tidy up the grain bins, scooping stray oats back onto the pile, so they aren't left behind. Toward noon, when I see him leaning on the gate at the barn, his eyes turned west, watching the mares and his stallion mingle, I know at this moment this life is enough for him.

Pete's always felt right if his hands did the work. A rancher nearby, Bill Higby, who ranches because he loves the life, not because he depends on it, once told Pete, "You know, I feel better at the end of the day if I've fixed a fence or moved some water in my meadows than I did when I sat at a desk." Later that day, Pete said to me, "I agree with Bill. I'm satisfied when I can actually see what I've done."

As I understand Pete's need to work with his hands, I understand that labor is satisfying when it's visible, when it counts for something in one's own environment. In generations gone by, most all work was physical work. And there was ownership and pride in what one created. Whether or not our children choose to work as Pete has done, I feel grateful for the hours they've spent building or fixing the next project, like the year Andy needed a feeder for his first 4-H pig.

When he was ten, Andy bought his first weaner pig for the fair. Every spring 4-H kids comb the want ads and inquire at the Extension Office about where they can buy weaner pigs weighing thirty to forty pounds; any more or less, and the pig may not make the right weight for market. The timing of buying in the spring gives the pigs fourteen weeks to reach market weight, anywhere from 180 to 260 pounds, before the fair. The competition for good livestock at the fair is fierce, so everyone is searching for the best breeders of show pigs.

That first pig was a Hampshire piglet. Andy purchased it from a group of pigs our 4-H agent, Jim Stanko, purchased from a regional producer. When Andy and I arrived at the Stanko Ranch, a squealing piglet pandemonium besieged us from the stock trailer. Jim hopped out of the truck and said, "Jump in there Andy, and grab yourself one." Andy's eyes widened as the uncontrolled squealing created a rapidly rising trepidation over stepping into the trailer and claiming his pig. He had to be quick to pick up a weaner pig by its bionic hind legs. Once the piglet was in his grasp, he faced a porcine battle: the hind legs a flurry of fury, defending against Andy's death grip. With a little help from Jim and me, Andy put his new charge in a burlap bag, tied a good knot in the top, and put it in the back of the pickup.

On the way home that day, Andy spilled all the details of the drama out into the cab of the pickup. This story would be told again and, in the telling, become a larger tale. But on that day, a ten-year-old had entered a trailer thundering with frightened piglets and in doing so, not only came out alive, but perhaps a little sturdier.

Pete called Andy out to the barn and said, "You know, you better be thinking about where you're gonna keep this pig. I had an idea. I'll show you here out back of the barn. We can put in some extra plywood and wire down here, so it can't get out. It can get down to the river, but we'll just have to keep an eye on it when the runoff comes. And I thought you could just use this leftover calf shelter with some straw in it. The one thing we don't have is a feeder, and I think they're pretty expensive if you buy one. You know that'll eat up your profits, so I think you better figure out how to make one."

Andy and Pete spent the better part of the morning raking through leftover plywood, looking for enough pieces the right size to put a feeder together. Most pig feeders are made out of tin, but plywood will work just fine. So the guys started measuring and cutting, following basic directions from Andy's livestock manual.

I wandered out to the shop in the late morning to check in. As I walked into the shop, I found Andy at the work bench, fitting two sides of the feeder together, securing them with screws. His next job would be to attach the lid. Pete showed him some old leather he could cut hinges from, so the lid opened and closed easily. The pig would put his snout under the lip of the lid and push it open. When he finished, the lid would close and protect the feed from both the birds and the weather.

Andy asked me, "Hey, Mom, what do you think?" "Looks good to me. I hope that little piglet appreciates his custom feeder." Pete followed with, "Ya, this is gonna be the Cadillac of feeders before we're through." Andy smiled and turned back to the work bench.

The two guys stopped briefly for a sandwich and then returned to the shop. Their collaboration continued through most of the afternoon, one measuring and one cutting. When they finished, Andy called me out to take a look and said, "Hey, Mom, could you take a picture of me with my feeder? I'm 'spose to have one for my 4-H record book."

When the picture was developed, I put it carefully away in his record book. I can still remember the gray sweatshirt, black Wranglers, and cowboy hat Andy wore that day. I can remember his smile in the picture, his hand over the top of the storage bin, and the look in his eyes—proud of his labor and of his accomplishment. In the end, the picture was a reminder that in the doing, in the making, in the piecing together of plywood, he experienced himself in relationship to his father, inside his father's workshop.

In the years ahead, we'd often find Andy out with his pigs, spraying them with a water bottle to keep them cool, scratching their ears, or just sitting in the straw visiting. The relationship with animals, his pigs, his dogs, and later on, his horses, would be as central to his daily life as it was for his father.

Now in his twenties, Andy discussed and planned breeding programs for our mares the other day with Pete. They rode and trained horses in the summer and debated the best way to get a young horse to flex in the neck or move its hind quarter. They planned and built fence from leftover oil pipe and finished up the new horse shed filling it with four inches of fine sand and hand painting the trim.

Just as his father had, Andy would find challenge, satisfaction, and personal ownership of success and failure with the building, the maintaining, and the artistry he felt in that which he created with his hands. It would be there that he would find evidence, not just of his labor, but of his existence.

Winter

Quilting Cattlewomen

Quilting Cattlewomen
Counter-clockwise from left, Sue Fulton, Michelle McKee,
Judy Green, Mary Kay Monger, Becky Appel, Laurie Hallenbeck,
Judy Brim, the author, and Betsy Blakeslee

Chapter Twenty-Three

Quilting Cattlewomen

February's full moon hangs high. At such a distance, its soft light reaches out and sets a silver-sequined meadow on stage. How clear the world outside my window when the moon hangs high in the sky. How clear the questions in my life become when time and distance travel through the night.

Winter 2006

L ast night, February's full moon filled my rear view mirror as I drove to the Carpenter Ranch to work on a quilt with other Cattlewomen. Our Routt County Cattlewomen's Association works hard to raise money for scholarships, supporting local youth in higher education. The quilt we're making will be raffled off and the proceeds donated to the scholarship fund.

The inherent socialization of quilting together mirrors quilt making history among ranching women. Between the mid-nineteenth century and the early twentieth century, women, whether they settled on the Great Plains or in the West, collaboratively practiced the art of quilt making. Often called "Quilting Bees," these gatherings brought women, physically isolated from one another, together for socialization and the practical work of making coverings for beds. The quilts were "pieced"—the quilt top designed, cut, and assembled—in the winter months, and the quilt quilted in the summer months when it could be set up outside on a large wooden quilt frame.

Quilt making on the plains or in a ranch house was never a singular act, but the threading of a community of hands linking each one to a greater societal kinship. Handmade quilts were used by the quilters themselves, given to brides, and offered for auctions at community fund-raising events, just as the Cattlewomen's quilt would be next fall.

When we meet, we set up our sewing machines and lay out our fabric on tables in a large room of the old Carpenter Ranch house. The room is used by the Nature Conservancy, which owns and operates the ranch, for educational events. The Nature Conservancy purchased the ranch in 1994 from the Ferry Carpenter family. Ferry, a lawyer from back East, started the ranch in 1930. Over the course of his lifetime, he served as a state legislator and contributed innovative thinking to grazing policies, water rights, and performance testing in cattle.

The Nature Conservancy chose the Carpenter Ranch to create a model for the coexistence of ranching and conservation. The Conservancy found a vibrant habitat along the banks of the Yampa River, rich in hay and alfalfa meadows. The Conservancy conducts extensive research on weeds, riparian habitat, and bird species on the ranch in addition to providing comprehensive educational programs for county schools and the general public.

One of our Cattlewomen helps run the Conservancy and offers the room in the old ranch house for our project. The Cattlewomen gathered around two long tables, spaced out perfectly, two women to a side. I sat next to Judy Green, a former school teacher and ranch wife, which really means she's a rancher.

She lost her right index finger to a team roping accident, and when she's not dressed up to represent her beloved Hayden Museum, she's in Wranglers.

Judy and her husband, Jerry, came home in 1980 to run the family ranch, when Jerry's parents could no longer manage on their own. Her husband's family homesteaded the place south of Hayden in 1895. Recently, the Colorado Master Farm Homemakers Guild recognized Judy as the "Homemaker of the Year," an antiquated title for someone who really makes her living off the ranch and contributes to the industry. It is difficult now to find these women ranchers to honor because it is so difficult to persevere in the strong winds of ranching hardships and to make a ranch truly financially viable.

Last night, we set out to sew a zillion squares together to make star blocks for the quilt. Judy and I brought our sewing machines, both Singers: hers, an 80s model, and mine, a 1947 Featherweight I'd just purchased on eBay. Most all the women know about the 1947 Featherweight, the old little workhorse of domestic sewing. They also remembered a time when they sewed on one. Mary Kay, our quilt project leader, taught her son and daughter on one because it was small and manageable. She said, "The best part was that it only went forward and backward." She laughed, knowing the mothers around her remembered teaching their children something and that keeping it simple made the difference between success and failure.

As Mary Kay reminisced, I remembered sitting and sewing in front of my mother's Singer, comfortable, at home. And then, I was in my grandmother's basement with Cassidy playing on the floor, watching my grandmother thread her sewing machine, a Featherweight she used until she died at ninety.

My grandmother's been gone twenty years, but I remembered her picking up fabric squares cut from donated odds and ends. As I sat near her, she explained what the squares were for. "You know, the people in nursing homes get cold when they sit in their wheelchairs, so they've asked our circle to donate lap robes. I think I've made over eighty by now. People send me the craziest leftover fabric. You wouldn't believe it, Mary. But it keeps me busy in the winter. You know, it can get so cold and dreary outside here in Cheyenne." Her hands continued pushing the fabric through her Singer, stitching one square to another until the quilt became a gift to lay over the lap of the receiver, a reminder that someone knew the chill of a Wyoming winter always seeped inside the nursing room walls.

Now sitting in front of a Singer in the old Carpenter Ranch, I filled the bobbin, remembering how my fingers moved around the machine as a young girl. Once it was threaded, I placed the small light beige and blue quilt squares under the zipper foot, pressed the rectangular pedal, and the dependable, regular straight stitch united square after square.

Next to me, Connie Wagner arranged the squares and handed them to me ready to sew. Connie comes from old time ranching. Her father, Perley Green, homesteaded with his family in the Twentymile Park area, near Fish Creek, in 1934. Then in 1941, they moved to a ranch property on Trout Creek in South Routt County where Perley settled in and would eventually bring his wife, Bonnie, to live with him in 1948. When Perley walked into the grocery store, everyone recognized his gray cowboy hat marked with sweat and dented from a life of work. Connie takes after her father: independent and dependable. She drives a school bus like he did and substitutes for the rural mail drivers. She always takes good care of our mail on Saturdays.

When I see Connie in the grocery store or with other Cattlewomen, she says, "How's that boy of yours? Behavin' himself? He's still ridin' those wild horses? You know these young people have to go out and do these things, Mary. But golly, I wish my girls would come around more often."

Connie treated Andy like her son. She watched him raise pigs and steers in 4-H and drove him on more than one school bus to wrestling tournaments and soccer games. She pulled his ear at the Fair and told him not to stay out too late: her own friendly reminder that 4-H officers need to set an example.

Last night, Connie needed to get out of the house. Her husband, Dan, was losing his battle with cancer and she had lost her mother, Bonnie, two years ago and her father a year ago. I think she collapsed for awhile in the depths of her grief. So, a dear friend invited her to come quilting, to take a rest from the heartbreak. Perhaps for a brief time she could find some peace in the movement of her hands, in the piecing of the quilt squares and surrounded by those who knew it was a good sign she was with us.

With two sewing machines whirring, two hands ironing, four hands arranging squares, and four hands trimming, we assembled half the star blocks. The zillion squares, when pieced together, will frame forty-one county ranch brands, embroidered in black on red cotton cloth. Some lucky ticket holder will take it home. Who will it be? Shouts from around the table went, "Ah, it's mine, it's mine. The rest of you don't have a chance." "No way. That quilt belongs on my bed. It's got my name written all over it." We all laid claim and threatened to buy not five, not ten, but twenty or more chances at a dollar each.

Stories of old quilts, of mothers teaching daughters to sew, and pants that needed to be patched over and over again, made an airline route map in Ferry Carpenter's old house. We repeated our gathering, sharing, and sewing ritual through May. The quilt had to be ready to travel around the county during the summer months, advertising the scholarship fundraiser. It hung in banks, the museum, and then in the Exhibit Hall at the Fair for ten days.

We entered our work in the quilt competition, joining everyone else who celebrates their harvest by bringing a jar of jam, a can of peaches, a fresh loaf of bread, a photograph of a grandchild, a miniature bouquet of pansies, fresh butter, home-brewed beer, a handmade rocking chair, or a wool suit. We joined in. We relished the gathering. We appreciated the hands that gave shape to the loaf of bread and the rocking chair, for in the making we knew that both the creator and the creation are brought to life, just as we had been brought to life in the presence of one another's company while cutting, piecing, and sewing our quilt.

In a twinkling, the buzz traveled through the Cattlewomen's e-mails. Our quilt had won a Grand Champion ribbon in the category of collaboratively created quilts. One by one, we savored our quilt showered in blues and purples as though western royalty slipped through the exhibits while we slept: the ribbons, etched in gold, echoing a community approbation for our effort, our care, our creativity.

Throughout the fall, the jars continued to fill with chance tickets. We chatted with old neighbors as they came by our table in the grocery store. They found change and bought one, two, maybe five tickets. Others passed by and said, "I've already bought twenty dollars worth, but I'm gonna keep buyin'. I want that quilt." Then just before Christmas, the local western store hosted our drawing at their midnight Christmas sale.

The winning ticket belonged to a long-time ranching family. They were familiar with some of the brands and the families who own them and use them and with some of the Cattlewomen who imagined, planned, and stitched the quilt. We, like the many women of the Great Plains and West, had repeated the threading and tying of community and kinship, the quilt, a visible reminder that our rural neighborhood still lives on.

Winter

Tracking Footprints

Snowshoe tracks on the TV tower hill

Chapter Twenty-Four

Tracking Footprints

Behind the burgundy window blind, the full "snow moon" reminds me of a southwestern cross on a New Mexico license plate. The fuzziness around the edges makes me impatient. I want the clarity of transparency. I want to know whether or not someone's telling me the truth.

-Winter 2006

The clock inched toward noon. I needed to get out of the house and onto the snowshoe trail. The walls close in come late February, and my mind and body seek renewal in exercise's deep breathing and winter's biting chill.

I started out across the meadows behind the house and quickly looked down to check my miniature canister of mace. Our old renter, Kirby, once told me I should carry a pistol when I ran or snowshoed up the nearby hill we call the TV tower (because of its outdated signal equipment). "You know we still see mountain lion and bear tracks around here. I always carry one when Dottie and I go up there after dinner. You should, too."

I recoiled at the thought of packing a gun in my Camelbak but told Kirby I'd give it some thought. When I think of handguns, I think of blood and guts and unsustainable solutions. But when I think of mountain lions and bears, I know there's a certain reality where the wild and primordial cross the path of trusting naiveté. Since Kirby's warning, I've continued to settle my dilemma with my mini-can of mace.

Striding out across the meadow, I watched for animal tracks and imagined the stories they might tell. One set of tracks looked like a fox trotting along, then stopping to circle and pounce, perhaps in search of a vole, and then trotting off as though he was headed home from school. Just before I crossed the road to the base of the hillside, his tracks disappeared.

Then my heart quickened as I stemmed the rise of the hill's access road with a snowshoe lockstep. With each breath I drew in, the salve of a fresh chilly breeze softened the tightness of a morning of sorting, shuffling, and settling words on the page. The few tracks I followed looked old, softened, and curled, like cookies in the oven when they rise and then fall just before a timer sounds. I was surprised to see so little wildlife activity. Grouse, squirrels, deer, elk, bluebirds, finches, ermine, fox, coyotes, bear, and mountain lion call the hillside home, and recently we've heard reports of wolves coming down from Wyoming.

Once resting at the spring, a point about three-fourths of the way up the hillside, I saw another set of fresh tracks and imagined that whatever it was, perhaps fox or coyote, smelled my scent from below and quickly went ahead. The lone set of tracks crossed the trail and headed up over the ridge where much of the wildlife seeks shelter in the aspens and pines.

In a minute or two, I heard a great howling just to the northwest. It seemed unusual, and in an instant I hoped it came from coyotes. The thought of coyotes during the day isn't as disturbing as the idea of a pack of wolves already this far south. I knew my mini-mace canister would pale in the face of neighborhood bullies.

I wanted to continue on to the top, but struggled with shrinking from the howling and from my disquiet. Halfway up, when the howling continued, I gave into the impulse to flee and headed down through an oak brush shortcut. As much I tried to enjoy a snowshoe freefall through the deep powder, a lump in my throat hijacked my *joi de vivre*.

I knew Pete would think I was silly if I told him what happened. Protecting myself, I saved the tale for later in the week, as time and distance seem to bring a crisis into focus, allowing for my own forgiveness of the fear and the impulse to flee.

During lunch a few days later, I asked Pete, "So do you think a bunch of coyotes would attack me up on the hill?"

"I don't know. You didn't run into a pack did you?" And without hesitation he added, "You know they've sighted the first wolf that's come down from Wyoming. You don't think that's what you heard?"

"I didn't think the howling sounded deep enough, like really scary, but it was different from anything I've heard."

Then in a surprisingly serious tone, he said, "I don't know what they'd do, but I think you're probably OK."

I was called to attention by his response. Pete didn't think I was silly. Then I reassessed how far my can of pepper spray would go on a pack of coyotes. Would it be enough to tag and turn the lead coyote back? Then would I have enough left for one or two more? And my then my mind refused to entertain mini-mace strategies for a pack of wolves, just as I had refused Kirby's handgun suggestions.

My conversation with Pete ended where it had begun: not knowing what the truth really was. I continued to snowshoe during the winter despite a day of howling and questions about wolves migrating. My feet must move when the walls close in, even though the wild has inhabited and will always inhabit our unassuming hill.

The modest summit, about eight hundred feet above the road, once sputtered and spewed from fault lines traveling beneath the valley. Plutonic rock litters its upper slope. In the summer, my feet step carefully on the rough remnants in six, eight, ten, and twelve inch chunks. Another million years away from soft and round, I'm bewildered by its geological youth.

Each time I summitted, I realized I'm both torn down and built back up again as I reached for air. One minute I can no longer push the limits, and in the next, I'm victorious over physical struggle and psychological doubt. Relieved, I stand to look north where the continental divide becomes the Zirkel Wilderness Area. In early June, I see vestiges of the last chilly season where the raw and the wild kill. Then in July, at summer's height, I reach out to the craggy divide, and my imagination soars with possibility.

Like an Indian scout, I repeated my scan of the valley, marking the geographical touch points below: Long Gulch, Deep Creek, Smith Creek, Wolf Mountain, and two ancient volcanic peaks, Pilot Knob, and Hahn's Peak. I toured the river bottom by following the stands of cottonwoods winding their way down the valley. The fence lines crisscrossed the meadows, and the irrigation ditches made squiggly lines down the middle of the pastures. Some houses were clustered as though gathered for warmth and others stood alone, in isolation or perhaps independence. I recited the landscape like a child reads her favorite story over and over again, and in doing so, masters what she sees and hears.

The Elk River Valley has held many in its fold. Whether clustered together for communion or isolated in self-determination, pioneers, new and old, put down roots in hope of a nurturing a productive life along its river bottom. Some succeeded and thrived; others met with adversity and misfortune. Tracking the footprints of those who came before offers rural and community members, as well as newcomers, added richness to their daily living. Richard L. Knight, in *Ranching West of the 100th Meridian,* believes it is true that "getting to know your human and natural history is essential to living well on a place." If we, new and old alike, come to this place because we are stirred by its physical and inspiring perspective, what else would one want to know?

I wondered, too, will newcomers put down roots in communion or isolation? In "Life in Paradox: Values, Environment, and Development in the American West," William Riebsame questions this relationship and draws the reader to a hopeful conclusion: "What should be our relationship to each other? Shall it continue to be one of dominance among social and economic classes? Colonization? Power struggles? Or is it to be one of cooperation and collaboration?"

Luther Propst, in his work as Executive Director of the Sonoran Institute, follows by suggesting "community stewardship" is an empowering approach to the challenging problems in our western landscapes and communities. "The love of the landscape— whether you work it, whether you view it on weekends, whether you move there in your retirement years to enjoy it passively—can unite people with disparate ideologies."

Come spring, as the snow cover on the nearby volcanic rise begins to slide and seep, and the snowdrops and glacial lilies unfold at its feet, I hope those who call this Valley home—Junior and his two boys, descendents of the Normans and Mays, Pete and me—as well as those new to the land, will join in our collective love and inspiration of this western landscape. If cool abundant waters, fertile meadows, plentiful grazing lands, wildlife habitats, and cultural historic landscapes are to survive, newcomers and conservators of working landscapes and open lands will need to walk with one another, our footprints soft and mutable. Then, just as the sandhill cranes take a southerly wing come fall and return to our meadows each spring, just as the shoal and the magma shift beneath our feet and the river bottom endures, just as the wolf may migrate to and fro, and just as our children take their leave and Pete and I remain, there will be a steadfastness beneath the change, ensuring our Elk River Valley remains the source of our collective sustenance and inspiration.

~~~~~~

Just as I paused for an interlude of writing and remembering, I will now place a bookend to the past and place a new one to mark the journey after midlife. For in the reflecting, I have unearthed what is most precious in my life through the stories between those bookends: the memories of raising our children, the sustenance found in friends and family, the value of community in our rural neighborhood, and the nurturing relationship found in the dynamic landscape of the Elk River Valley. Now gathered and preserved, these stories will enlighten and comfort in the days ahead.

Afterword

In the years since I finished writing the essential content of this book, Andy and Cassidy transitioned into adulthood. The questions their father and I asked ourselves and I posed in my writing during those years after they left home now have answers, at least for now. We wondered, "Would they be successful in finding careers related to the world of agriculture?"

Andy graduated from Cal Poly in 2003 with a degree in Agricultural Business in International Marketing. After competing on the pro rodeo circuit for three years, Andy trained two-year olds for the cutting horse industry outside Fort Worth, Texas. He now trains performance quarter horses through his business, *Andy Kurtz Performance Horses,* headquartered in Steamboat Springs, Colorado. In addition to his training business, he hosts horsemanship clinics including the *Common Ground Riding Clinic* with Regina Wendler, an English riding instructor. This clinic offers participants an in-depth look at the commonalities of eastern and western riding traditions. As part of his love of horse training and competition, Andy competes each year in National Reined Cow Horse Association events on both the regional and national level.

Cassidy graduated from Colorado State University with a double major in Animal Science and Agricultural Business in 2006. She completed her Master's Degree from Texas A&M in Equine Exercise Physiology in 2009. Before graduating, she participated in the American Quarter Horse European Horse Expos conducting horsemanship clinics in

Sweden, Denmark, and Germany. She now serves as the Routt County 4-H Youth Extension Agent in Steamboat Springs, Colorado. She continues to take time to train her own barrel horses and offers seminars on equine nutrition, performance, and training. Cassidy also designs and sells custom western jewelry through her business, *Jewels West.*

Pete and I continue to operate our ranch. We carry a small herd of cattle each summer, hay the river bottom, and raise performance quarter horses. The natural rhythms and cycles of the ranching seasons continue to provide a rich backdrop for our lives. The spring and summer seasons are demanding with fencing, irrigating, haying, general maintenance of the gardens, landscape, and equipment, overseeing the daily needs of livestock, and working with young horses in training. The days are long with the dinner hour late, but a sense of satisfaction seeps in deeply at the end of the day.

I appreciate perhaps more than ever the community in which we live: the long-held relationships, the support and encouragement with those with whom we work, and the values of a community that, albeit with certain frustrations and challenges, work toward the ideal of a sustainable environment. Although the pressures of development on rural lands continue, local efforts to support conservation easements in our county have preserved approximately 15,000 acres of open lands since 2006. Pete and I will always feel grateful to those who continue to work toward preserving the nourishing and inspiring landscape of this place we call home.

BIBLIOGRAPHY

A Western Horseman Book. *Legends: Outstanding Quarter Horses Stallions and Mares.* Colorado Springs, Colo.: Western Horseman Incorporated, 1983.

Boeree, George C. "Victor Frankl: 1905-1997." Pages 1-11. Retrieved March 2, 2006, <www.ship.edu/~cgboeree/frankl.html>.

"Boston Terriers." Pages 1-4. Retrieved September 9, 2006 <http://en.wikikpedia.org/w/index.php?title = Boston_Terrier&printable=yes>.

Chavez, Donald Gilbert Y. "Cowboys-Vaqueros: Origins of the First American Cowboys." Chapter 2. Retrieved February 10, 2006, <www.parrotshorse chat.com/Parrots_Perch/mailinglist/chap2.html>.

Jefferson, Thomas (1784). Excerpts from the book *Notes on the State of Virginia.* Avalon Project at Yale Law School. Retrieved November 17, 2005 <www.yale.edu/lawweb/avalon/jevifram.htm>.

Knight, Richard, Wendell C. Gilgert, and Ed Marston, editors. *Ranching West of the 100th Merdian: Culture, Ecology, and Economics.* Washington: Island Press, 2002.

Lyons, John. *Lyons on Horses: John Lyon's Conditonal-Response Training Program.* New York, N.Y.: Doubleday, 1991.

Main-Winogrosky, Kathy. *Early History of Clark, Colorado.* Clark, Colo.: Clark Cemetery Association, 2001

Parelli, Pat. *Natural Horse-Man-Ship.* Colorado Springs, Colo.: Western Horsemanship Inc., 1993.

Propst, Luther . "Healthy Landscapes, Vibrant Economies, and Livable Communities: Envisioning a West that Works." March 14, 2002. Retrieved October 13, 2006, <www.uwyo.edu/enr/ienr/DistinguishedSpeakers/Propst14March2002.asp>.

Riebsame, William E.. "*Life in Paradox Valley: Values, Environment, and Development in the American West.*" 1993. Retrieved October 9, 2006, <www.angelo.edu/events/university_symposium/1993/riebsame.htm>.

Stevenson, Thelma. *Historic Hahns Peak.* Fort Collins, Colo.: Robinson Press, Hahn's Peak Historical Society, Inc., 1976.

The International Museum of the Horse. "The Legacy of the Horse." Chapter 1C. Retrieved January 27, 2006 <www.imh.org/imh/kyhpllc.html>.

Suggested Reading

Alanen, Arnold and Robert Melnick. *Preserving Cultural Landscapes in America.* Baltimore, Md.: The Johns Hopkins University Press, 2000.

Best, Allen. "How does snow melt? A test for all Westerners." *High Country News.* February 18, 2002,

page 1. Retrieved February 23, 2006 <www.
hcn.org/servlets/hcn.PrintableArticle?article_id=
11031>.

Brown, Margaret Duncan. *Shepherdess of the Elk River Valley*. Denver, Colo.: Golden Press, 1967.

Campion, Lynn. *Behind the Scenes at America's Most Exciting Sport*. Guilford, Conn.: Lyons Press Imprint of the Globe Pequot Press, 2002.

Clayton, John. "For Western myths, see newcomers on horseback." *High Country News*. March 1, 2004,page 1. Retrieved February 23, 2006 <www.hcn.org/servlets/hcn.PrintableArticle?artic le_id=14614>.

Clifford, Hal. "Rancher's new cash crop will be scenery." *High Country News*. November 27, 1995, page 1. Retrieved February 23, 2006 <www. hcn.org/servlets/hcn.PrintableArticle?article_id= 1470>.

Jenkins, Matt. "Colorado River states reach landmark agreement." *High Country News*. February 20, 2006,page 1. Retrieved February 23, 2006 <www.hcn.org/servlets/hcn.PrintableArticle?artic le_id=16111>.

Limerick, Patricia Nelson. "Enduring Myths and Iconoclastic Realities." *The Colorado College State of the Rockies Project Challenge Talk*. April 4, 2005. Retrieved November 17, 2005 <www. coloradocollege.edu/stateoftherockies/05conference/ Limerick.htm>.

Marrin, Albert. *Cowboys, Indians, and Gunfighter: The Story of the Cattle Kingdom*. New York, N.Y.: Anthenum Publishers, 1993

Miller, Lyle. "Preserving Colorado's Agricultural History: Projects Exemplify State Historical Fund's Commitment to Saving Ranches and Farms." *Colorado History/Now* (January 2006):5.

Morgan, M.H., trans. "Xenophon." *The Art of Horsemanship*. London, Eng.: J.A. Allen and Company Limited, 1962.

Pritchett, Lulita Crawford. *Remembering the Old Yampa Valley*. Steamboat Springs, Colo.: NextPrint, LLC, 2005.

Smith, Claude A. Jr. and Kathy Main-Winogrosky. *The Life and Times of Sophia Norman Smith: A Clark, Colorado Pioneer Woman*. Clark, Colo.: Clark Cemetery Association, 1998.

Starrs, Paul. *Let the Cowboy Ride: Cattle Ranching in the American West*._Baltimore, Maryland: The Johns Hopkins University Press, 1998.

Taylor, Lonn and Ingrid Maar. *The American Cowboy*. Baltimore, Md.: Derek Birdsall and Garamond Pridemark Press, 1983.

Towler, Sureva and Jim Stanko. *Faster Horses, Younger Women, Older Whiskey: A Pictorial Archive of the Routt County Fair 1914-1995*. Steamboat Springs, Colo.: White River Publishing Company, 1996.

Tread of the Pioneers Museum. *The Historical Guide to Routt County*. Denver, Colo.: the author, 1979.

Resources

American Farm Land Trust
1200 18th NW Suite 800
Washington, D.C. 20036
www.farmland.org

Colorado Cattlewomen
http://yampavalley.info/centers/agriculture/
organizations/colorado_cattlewomen%252C_inc.

Colorado History Society
1300 Broadway
Denver, Colorado 80203
303-866-3682

Colorado Cattlemen's Association
Colorado Cattlemen's Agricultural Land Trust
8833 Ralston Road
Arvada, Colorado 80002
www.ccalt.org
303-431-6422

Community Agricultural Alliance
1370 Bob Adams Drive Suite 318
Steamboat Springs, Colorado 80487
970-879-4370
Executive Director: Marsha Daughenbaugh

Hayden Heritage Center Museum
300 W. Pearl
Hayden, Colorado 81639
970-276-4380
heritagemuseum@nctelecom.net

Land Trust Alliance
www.lta.org
Western Policy Director: Lynne Sherrod

The Nature Conservancy
P.O. Box 775528
Steamboat Springs, Colorado 80477
970-879-1546
Regional Director: Geoff Blakeslee

Tread of Pioneers Museum
P.O. Box 772372
Steamboat Springs, Colorado 80477
970-879-2214

Yampa Valley Information Project
www.yampavalleyinfo.org

Yampa Valley Land Trust
P.O. Box 773014
Steamboat Springs, Colorado 80477
970-8797240
Director: Susan Otis

Publications

High Country News: *For People Who Care About the West*
P.O. Box 1090
Paonia, Colorado 81428
www.hcn.org

Farm and Ranch Living: For Families Who Love the Land
5925 Country Lane
Greendale, Wisconsin 53129
www.farmandranchliving.com

<u>Links</u>

www.marybkurtz.com
www.marybkurtz.blogspot.com
www.kurtzranch.com
www.andykurtz.com
www.jewelswest.com

Index

About the Author

Mary Kurtz and her husband raise cattle, hay, and quarter horses on their ranch in the Elk River Valley in northwestern Colorado. The mother of two adult children, she has contributed to *Farm and Ranch Living,* the *Trail Rider Magazine, Country Woman* and *Cats and Kittens.* Join Mary on her website at: www.marybkurtz.com

CPSIA information can be obtained at www.ICGtesting.com
Printed in the USA
LVOW061952011211

257475LV00001B/4/P